THE PROFIT EQUATION

THE PROFIT EQUATION

Achieving Success through Measurement

Michael D. Batt

THE PROFIT EQUATION
Achieving Success through Measurement

Copyright © 2011, 2013 by Michael D. Batt

All rights reserved. No part of this book may be used or reproduced by any means, graphic, electronic, or mechanical, including photocopying, recording, taping or by any information storage retrieval system without the written permission of the publisher except in the case of brief quotations embodied in critical articles and reviews.

The information, ideas, and suggestions in this book are not intended to render professional advice. Before following any suggestions contained in this book, you should consult your personal accountant or other financial advisor. Neither the author nor the publisher shall be liable or responsible for any loss or damage allegedly arising as a consequence of your use or application of any information or suggestions in this book.

iUniverse books may be ordered through booksellers or by contacting:

iUniverse
1663 Liberty Drive
Bloomington, IN 47403
www.iuniverse.com
1-800-Authors (1-800-288-4677)

Because of the dynamic nature of the Internet, any web addresses or links contained in this book may have changed since publication and may no longer be valid. The views expressed in this work are solely those of the author and do not necessarily reflect the views of the publisher, and the publisher hereby disclaims any responsibility for them.

Any people depicted in stock imagery provided by Thinkstock are models, and such images are being used for illustrative purposes only.
Certain stock imagery © Thinkstock.

ISBN: 978-1-4620-2862-7 (sc)
ISBN: 978-1-4620-2860-3 (e)
ISBN: 978-1-4620-2861-0 (hc)

Library of Congress Control Number: 2011909963

Printed in the United States of America

iUniverse rev. date: 4/2/2013

To my family

Introduction

In the world of sports, statistics reign supreme. Ask any true baseball fan, and he could rattle off an assortment of "stats" for his favorite player, such as batting average, runs batted in, total batters faced, stolen base percentage, home runs, earned run average, just to name a few.

Hours, weeks, months, and even careers have been devoted to the development, tracking, and analyzing of sports statistics. Players live and die by them. Fans devour morning newspapers, reliving yesterday's games through the statistics.

While sports statisticians are busy measuring pitches, shots, yards, and runs, business managers around the world are engaged in a very similar activity—trying to measure business performance. They measure cost per call, average sale, return on investment, units produced per man hour ...

Just as in sports, many employees live and die by their stats. They are promoted, given bonuses, and even fired based on their abilities to "put up good numbers." Managers rehash their departments' statistics daily, weekly, monthly, and annually. They post them on walls in break rooms, brag about them in staff meetings, and report on them in performance reviews.

This method of management, often called "management by measurement," is a powerful tool to help drive the performance of a business ... if done correctly.

Over many years and in many different roles—including controller, vice president, and general manager of the Utah Jazz's Retail Division and chief operating officer and general manager of

Riverbend Holdings, a company with operations in ranching, real estate investments, radio broadcasting, construction, and title insurance—I have repeatedly had the eye-opening realization that all of our measuring didn't always get us where we wanted to be.

Through the years, we would often measure one aspect of a business, hoping to drive improvements, only to find that other areas of the business fell victim to neglect. We would then swing the pendulum and measure something new to correct for our earlier myopic focus. Subsequently, we would neglect the area that we had just fixed, letting it once again fall into disarray.

The cycle seemed to be endless. We were constantly fighting fires and trying to find the right measurements and a method of applying them that would help us reach our ultimate goal. It was tiring and often felt self-defeating.

And then it began to click. Not all at once, but gradually. With endless hours at a whiteboard, many long days, and the support of countless colleagues, friends, and mentors, a process came to life—a way to identify the few key measurements that really mattered and the method to make those measurements drive change.

The process was revitalizing. It gave new life to work and made going to the office each morning a joy. Profits improved dramatically, and even more importantly, employees began to love their jobs again. We were able to engage our employees, improve our decision making, and ultimately reach our goals.

Written in an easy-to-read novel style, *The Profit Equation* will teach you this process. It will change the way you look at problems and empower you to go out and accomplish your goals.

So sit back and enjoy, and then get up and make it happen!

Chapter 1

Could the clock really move that slowly? It's Monday and only fifteen minutes into algebra, and it feels like time is standing still! Why did a decent guy like Coach Hunter—or Coach H. as the guys call him—ever decide to teach algebra anyway? Here he is the coach of the high school baseball team, and he chose a geeky subject like math to teach. Why not something like PE that everyone could respect?

"Davis!"

Ouch. Where did that come from? Coach H. has a way with chalk erasers. If you aren't "in the game," as he calls it, you'll likely catch an eraser upside the head.

"Sorry, Coach," I mumble as I check for blood where the eraser hit the top of my head. Coach H. played baseball in college for a couple years. That was before he tore a rotator cuff and decided to teach math instead. He still throws a mean fastball though—or eraser, in this case. He won't stand for anyone dozing off or daydreaming in class. For some strange reason that no one can quite figure out, he is crazy about math—well, more specifically algebra.

"Listen, Davis. You've gotta get in the game. You miss order of operations, and you'll be treadin' water for the next six months. What's come over you lately? You've gotta focus."

"I know, I know. I'll do better," I say as I rub the bump that is forming on the top of my head.

The truth is, I'm having a hard time focusing on anything lately. Between work, school, basketball, and girls, nothing seems to be going right. I'd better not start on that now; gotta get back in the game.

"Okay class, back to order of operations," Coach H. continues. "Who can tell me which comes first when solving an equation: addition or multiplication?"

Of course Samantha Wilmington would raise her hand.

"Multiplication."

"That's right, Samantha. Good job. Now, how about subtraction or division?"

No one jumps at this one, not even Samantha. Another of the great mysteries of the universe—even more puzzling than Coach H.'s obsession with algebra—is how did a cute girl like Samantha Wilmington get so good at math? She even seems to like it. Seriously, who likes math? And how is Samantha ever supposed to dig a kid like me who barely passed geometry in the ninth grade?

"Come on, guys. Somebody give it a shot," Coach H. prods.

What the heck.

"How about division?" I guess timidly.

"Is that a question or an answer, Davis? You've got to say it like you mean it: division!" Coach H. says as he pounds on his desk. "That's right. Division."

"You've got to remember three key rules," he continues. "First, anything within parentheses happens first. Second, multiplication and division always happen before addition and subtraction. Finally, once the first two rules have been satisfied, you work from left to right—just like reading a book."

How am I ever going to use this in real life, I think as I lean back in my chair and stretch my legs out under my desk. I can see how I might use the things I am learning in English, my first class of the day. I'll surely need to write and communicate clearly. Auto body, my second class, is a fun class and has always been intriguing to me. My third class of the day, PE, is at least fun if not useful for life. After algebra, my fourth class, I have Spanish and art. Given the huge population of Hispanics in our small town, Spanish is invaluable. Art, like auto body, is another hobby I really enjoy. All of the classes are at least potentially useful if not fun—all but algebra. It just doesn't connect in my mind how I can ever use all of these letters, numbers, and rules in life to help me accomplish anything.

Okay, I've gotta get back in the game.

Coach H. is going on about the order of operations.

"Let's do a practice problem guys," he says as I mentally join them again.

He writes on the board as he talks:

$$A \times (B + C) - D = E$$

$A = 4$
$B = 3$
$C = 2$
$D = 6$

"What does E equal?" Coach asks as he finishes. This is his routine. He explains a concept, writes up a problem and then lets us try it out.

Now what did he say comes first? Oh yeah, multiplication. A times B would be 12. Then, going left to right: 12 plus 2 minus 6 equals 8. So E equals 8. I raise my hand.

Samantha, of course, already has her hand up. Coach H. calls on her, and she says "Fourteen."

"That's right, Samantha." Coach H. smiles.

Now, how in the world did she get 14?

Coach H. explains as I look back through my notes.

"Remember the rules: first, parentheses; second, multiplication and division; and third, left to right."

Oh yeah, parentheses first.

The rest of the class is a blur as Coach H. writes problems on the board and we work through them together. If this is all we have to do, I think I can handle it. Of course, we're only a few weeks into the semester, so chances are it's only getting tougher.

Michael D. Batt

I look back over at Samantha and see her working feverishly as Coach H. writes another equation on the board. We've been in the same classes since elementary school—though I'm not sure she knows that I exist—and for some reason, she's always had a way with math. I, on the other hand, just get by in math, at least passing so I can play sports but usually not much better. She will probably go on to be some famous scientist or mathematician. I don't aspire to anything like that. I guess I've decided that business would suit me better. I'm pretty good with people and enjoy selling things. We'll see. For now, I need to figure out a way to pass algebra so I can finish out the basketball season.

The bell finally rings, and I pack up my books to head for the door. As I make my way through the desks, Coach H. catches up with me.

"Davis!"

"Yeah, Coach?"

"Can you swing by after school today?" he asks. "We need to talk."

"Sure," I say as I head out the door.

Great, just what I need—another pep talk from the math teacher. It's the same every year. About a week or two into class, the teacher pulls me aside and gives me the same "You know, if you applied yourself…" speech. It's not that I'm a bad student; I just don't really care for math.

CHAPTER 2

Spanish and art creep by like an old freight train headed for a brick wall. Any time a teacher asks you to come talk after school … well, let's just say there are things I'd rather do with my afternoon. As the hallways clear out, I make my way back toward the math room. I have to wait outside for a minute while Coach H. finishes talking to another poor soul, probably practicing his speech for me.

Finally, after what seems like an eternity, it's my turn. Preparing for the worst, I knock on his office door.

"Coach, you wanted to talk to me?" I stick my head in the door as he cleans a few books off his desk.

"Yeah, come on in Davis," he says, and he points to a chair.

"Thanks," I mumble.

"So, how is the basketball season going this year? I came to the game last week. You played well, but you guys sure got licked by old Skyline," he says with a grin. He grins because he can. Last spring, the baseball team took state, beating "old" Skyline in the division championship.

"Yeah, it's been hit-and-miss this year. We've had a couple good games and then … well, a couple of games like last week. Not too consistent yet, but we're working on it."

It's the truth. We play well occasionally, but we can't do it on command, that's for sure.

"So," he continues, "tell me, what else is going on in life?"

I'll give him credit. Coach H. has a way of talking that puts you at ease and makes you feel like you can open up.

"I don't know. Things are good."

I'm pretty sure he wouldn't want to hear my sob story. What could a math teacher do, anyway, to solve a kid's problems?

"Well, I know something's eatin' at you. I've watched enough kids in class and on the team that I can tell when something's bothering a guy. You're not with us in class, and I know you're a bright guy."

Here it comes: the "You're a bright guy if you'd just apply yourself" speech.

When I don't respond, he continues, "You're probably thinking that I'm going to tell you that you just need to apply yourself. Don't worry, I'm not. I'm sure you've heard the 'apply yourself speech' before and don't want to hear it again."

I try to hide a smile. *He's good. It's like he sees right through me. Now that he's onto me, I guess there's no harm in telling him why I can't seem to stay in the game in class.*

Where to start? Work, school, basketball, girls—nothing seems to be going that well these days.

Coach beats me to it as I begin to open my mouth, "How's work these days? You work down at the mall, don't you?"

"Yeah, I got a job last spring at the sports store in the mall. I thought it would be a good fit for me. It's been pretty good, but my boss always seems to be on my case. He wrote me up last week for the second time—says my stats aren't good enough. One more write-up, and I'm out. I hustle, but it seems like the harder I work the worse my stats get. I'm not sure what to do. If I get fired, I'll be hard-pressed to find another job in the mall."

"So what kind of stats are they measuring?" Coach asks.

"Two, really. The first is *Average Sale*—overall sales divided by the number of transactions during a shift. The second is *Items per Transaction*—or *IPT*—the total number of items sold during a day divided by the number of transactions."

"Interesting." Coach leans back in his chair and puts his hands behind his head. Finally, he moves on. "Tell me about basketball. That's going pretty well, isn't it? You run point, right? Seems like you're the star of the show."

"I guess its okay. I've played pretty well, but we're struggling as a team. As the captain, the team is looking to me to turn things around, but I'm not sure where to start. We have a lot of talent but can't seem to put it all together on the floor. We'd love a shot at state but are on the brink of being out of the running."

Coach moves on, without commenting on what I said. "So I've seen you watching Samantha. She's a cute girl. Have you asked her out?"

"No way. I don't even think she'd go out with me if I asked. Anyway, I'm too busy with basketball and work and trying to stay on top of school. I don't have time for dates."

Another nice lie. If I thought I had a prayer, I'd give it a try, but I don't have the guts to get shot down by a girl like Samantha. I'd be the talk of the school.

"So what about school?" Coach asks. "I guess as a teacher I ought to ask about that too, right?"

"I guess so." I shrug. How can I tell him everything is going pretty well except algebra? I guess if anyone already knows, it's probably him.

"I'm doing okay in most of my classes, but algebra seems to be giving me a run for my money. I'm having a hard time getting how I'll ever use all these letters, numbers, and equations in real life. It's just not clicking for me."

"I know where you're coming from, Davis," Coach begins slowly. "You probably couldn't guess it now, but twelve or fifteen years ago, I was sitting in your shoes. I was hoping and praying that I could at least get a good enough grade to pass algebra so I could play baseball. The last thing on my mind was that someday I'd be an algebra teacher."

"So what flipped the switch for ya, Coach?" I ask, "I mean, you're great at math now. Especially algebra."

"That's a great question and even a better story, Davis. Probably too much for tonight. I'll tell you another time. You better get going to work so you're not late."

I grab my bag and stand up. As I reach for the door, Coach throws me a curve, "Listen, Davis. You may not buy this now, but I think I can help you with most of the problems you've talked about here. Believe it or not, algebra is more useful than you think. Come by tomorrow before school, and we can talk about it some more."

I thank him for his time and hustle down the hallway. I'm going to have to book it to get to work on time. The last thing I need is to be late. Luckily, I don't think Jimmy, my boss, is working tonight. That should give me some time to think about what I need to do to make sure I don't end up out of work and out of cash.

My old beater of a car is right where I left it this morning—unfortunately. I've often thought it would be nice if someone would steal it so my parents would let me get a new one. They always remind me though that a car is meant to get you from point A to point B, and as long as mine does that, I'm stuck with it. It's yet another reason that I have a hard time believing Samantha Wilmington would want to go out with me. What girl would want to be caught dead in a bright orange, beat-up El Camino?

I gun out of the parking lot, barely missing a driver's education car headed out for practice. That ought to give that freshman a rush.

As I jump on the road into town, I start thinking about Coach H.'s last comment. For the life of me, I can't imagine how algebra could solve any of my problems—let alone all of them. But if there is a secret that can get me a girlfriend, help me pass algebra, kick-start our basketball team, and salvage my job, I'm willing to give it a try. I don't believe it, but it can't hurt to hear him out.

I pull into the parking lot at the mall and start looking for a parking spot close to the entrance by our store. Some guys have all the luck, and I'm definitely not one of them. I make it to the store just in time. To my surprise, Jimmy is working tonight. He explains that the district manager—or DM as we call him—is coming by in the morning. Jimmy wants to clean up the store so it will be ready for the visit tomorrow.

The Profit Equation

I was hoping it would be a quiet night, but I know we've got our work cut out for us. Jimmy has been so focused on "stats" lately that we haven't done a great job of keeping the store clean.

Jimmy is a nice enough guy. He hired me to help out part-time in the evenings and on the weekends. At first, he was pretty cool, but as time has gone on, he's gotten more uptight about our stats. We have to report them nightly on the stat board in the backroom, and lately, my name has been sliding down the board. I'm sure the visit from the DM tomorrow won't help. It always seems like, for a few weeks after these visits, Jimmy gets more worked up about the stats.

Maybe it's because our store's been slipping a little the last few months compared to the other stores our DM manages. We're still one of the top stores in the company though, and I don't understand why everyone gets so worried about a few little numbers.

I head to the backroom to start straightening things up. At least I can't get into trouble for my stats being bad tonight. As long as I'm in the backroom, I won't have to sell, and I'll be off the hook. It might be my chance to think a little.

As I open the door to the backroom, I stop at the stat board. There they are: the two lists. One ranking all employees by *Average Sale*, and the other ranking all employees by *Items per Transaction* or *IPT*. Jimmy says these are the bread-and-butter of retail and that every retailer in the mall tracks these stats. He always says that if you can drive these two numbers, you can drive your business. I'm driving them all right—driving them right into the ground. I guess that's the problem.

I hang my jacket over the stat board so it won't remind me of my failure and get to work on cleaning up the backroom. By the time my shift is over, everything is organized, the floor is mopped, and all of the hangers and bags are stacked neatly in their bins.

I open the door and holler for Jimmy to come and check out my work. He and Larry are just finishing straightening the T-shirts on some shelves, and he says he'll be back in a minute.

When he finally comes, he's impressed with my work.

Michael D. Batt

"You know, Davis. If you could sell as well as you clean, we would be in business."

I guess that's supposed to be a compliment, so I thank him and head out of the store. It will be interesting to get the report on how the visit with the DM goes. I'll probably get the wrath on Wednesday, when I work again, for bringing down the store stats and making Jimmy look bad.

As I drive home, I start to think again about Coach's words—"you may not buy this now, but I think I can help you with most of the problems you've talked about here. Believe it or not, algebra is more useful than you think."

I have to admit, I'm interested.

Chapter 3

My alarm goes off Tuesday morning a few times before I finally manage to crawl out of bed. As I jump in the shower and turn on the water, I start to think again about what Coach H. could possibly have to say.

As usual, I feel like I could stand under the warm water forever, but I don't want to be late. I hurry to get ready for school and tell Mom that I'm skipping breakfast today. Of course, she puts up a fuss. She's old school—always insisting that breakfast is the most important meal of the day. Finally, she convinces me to take a bagel and banana to eat on the way.

I run out the door and fire up the El Camino. Who ever thought of making a car that doubles as a truck? And how did I end up driving one?

I pull into the parking lot before most of the kids are at school. At last, I get a good parking spot right near the walk up to the school. I hustle inside and make my way to Coach's classroom.

He's there, working away at something. He's got equations all over the board, and he looks like a kid in a candy store. I almost hate to break his concentration—like disturbing an artist at his canvas.

Finally, I speak up, "Hey, Coach. I came by like you asked."

"Oh, Davis. I'm glad you made it. I was wondering if you'd actually come," Coach says as he erases the board.

"Have a seat." He motions to a seat in the front row. He leans against the wall and puts his hands on his hips.

"So, have you thought about what I said last night? You know, that math could help you solve your problems?" Coach asks.

"Yeah, I've thought some. The problem is that I'm no good at math." I decide to tell it like it is: "I'm barely passing. If it gets any worse, I won't pass, and then I can't play ball. Math seems more like the problem right now than the answer. Believe me, if you can help, I'd love it, but I just don't see how algebra is going to make my life any better."

"I hear ya, Davis." Coach nods. "The problem is you don't see the vision of what math is really all about. I'm not saying that most of the kids in the class do. I know I didn't when I was in high school."

Math. Vision. He's right: I don't see the vision, if in fact there is one. I was hoping that this help would be a lot more straightforward, something like a promise that if I passed math he'd buy me a new car, get me a girlfriend, give me a job.... Unfortunately, it doesn't look like that's what he has in mind.

He continues, "Let's take algebra for example. What do you think about algebra?"

"I don't know," I mumble. "A bunch of letters and numbers, I guess. I'm just not sure what they have to do with real life."

"Do you know where algebra comes from, Davis?"

"No idea," I say coolly, trying to help him see that not only do I not know but that I really don't even care.

"Well, let's start there," Coach goes on, dismissing my disgruntled remark. He grabs a book off the shelf and flips through a few pages. "Here we go," he begins.

"There was a guy in Baghdad—that's over in the middle east—back about 1,200 years ago, who was one of the first to ever write about algebra. His name was Al-Khwarizmi." Coach points to the name in the book, admitting that he probably just butchered it.

"Instead of using letters like we use in class, he used words to represent the variables that he was trying to solve for. Around 825 AD, he wrote a book called *Al-jabr w'al muq abala*. That's where we get the term 'algebra.' The meaning of the word algebra is 'restoration of broken parts.'"

"'Restoration of broken parts,' huh? What does that mean?" I ask, trying not to seem too interested.

"Good question, Davis. Let's see if we can think of an example that might explain it a little better. Take a simple jigsaw puzzle—one that your little brother or sister might do. Say the completed, whole puzzle is represented by the letter E. Say there are four pieces in this puzzle that are represented by the letters A, B, C, and D. If you dump the puzzle out, you have a bunch of broken parts. As you put the pieces together, you are restoring these broken parts to become a whole picture again. In essence, we could say that $A + B + C + D = E$. The combination or restoration of the pieces creates the whole.

"Of course, the pieces have to go together in the right order. Even if you have all the pieces but stack them on top of each other, you wouldn't get the same result as if you put them together the way they were designed to go to make a picture."

Coach sets the book back on the shelf and sits in a desk next to me, letting me internalize what he's said.

The bell rings. I still feel like I need more explanation, but kids start to file in for first period.

As Coach goes to welcome his class, he looks back over his shoulder, "Come by again Thursday, and we'll keep working on it. Before too long, you'll see how it will help."

After I sit down in English, I think about our conversation. *Restoration of broken parts*. I definitely have broken parts in my life. Now the question is how to restore them.

I continue to think about it through the rest of English without really coming to any good conclusions.

During the next period—auto body—I'm pretty wrapped up in our project. This is my second year of auto body, so we actually get to do some cool stuff. We are working on restoring an old, 1968 Ford Mustang.

I wonder if the restoring that Coach is talking about is similar to what we are doing to this old car. On the wall, we have a big picture of the car—so we know what we want the car to look like when we are all done. Unfortunately, our car doesn't look anything like that now. It's got quite a few rust spots and dents.

I guess that's the fun of it, taking something that once was a piece of art and trying to put it back together again.

Restoration of broken parts—the phrase runs through my mind again and again. If I could do the same thing to my broken parts as we're doing to this car, life would be great.

I guess the only differences are that I don't think it will be quite as fun to fix up my life as it is to fix up the Mustang, and secondly, I don't have a clue where to start or how to do it.

Hopefully, Coach can help.

CHAPTER 4

Before I know it, school is out, and I've got basketball practice.

I usually work on Mondays and Saturdays and then one or two nights during the week after basketball practice. This week, I work again on Wednesday and then not again until Saturday.

"Hey, Davis," Slim hollers across the gym as I come in. His real name isn't Slim, but that's what the guys call him. He's really not that slim either at six feet one inch and 280 pounds. He's a real likeable guy and one of the best players on the team.

"Hey," I call back as I hurry into the locker room to get ready before practice starts.

We run through the same drills we do every practice—a dribbling drill, a passing drill, and a shooting drill. The guys go on autopilot as we run through the drills, spending most of the time complaining about the drills and asking when we can scrimmage. Wally, our coach, pushes us until he can't stand the griping anymore. Finally, he breaks down, and we spend most of the practice just playing "pick-up" style ball.

Wally, like my boss, seems to be all about the stats. It seems like my life is full of people who are wrapped up in measuring every little thing I do. Wally's favorites are shooting percentage and total rebounds. As a guard, I usually don't worry much about rebounds, but I really try to improve my shooting percentage. Slim and I usually take most of the shots, because we're the best shooters.

Wally also makes sure we push it hard. He believes in running, running, and more running. He always says we'll be in better shape than any team we meet on the hardwood. I believe him. By the end of the scrimmages, I can barely stand up. We can outrun most teams, but I sure wish we could win a few more games.

After we scrimmage for an hour or so, we call it a practice and head to the showers. As I stand under the warm water, I start thinking about the team. I can't seem to put my finger on the broken part in the team.

We've probably got some of the best talent in the district. Slim plays strong forward and will likely be all-state this year. I play point and seem to get the ball worked around to the open man pretty well. Charley is our big man underneath and can out-rebound almost anybody. Bill and Jeff are our other two starters. There's hardly a better starting lineup out there.

Thinking back to Coach H.'s puzzle analogy this morning, I feel pretty confident that we have the right pieces; I wouldn't pick anybody else to play with. I'm pretty sure we are putting the pieces together correctly. I know I couldn't play center, and I'm pretty sure Slim would never make much of a point guard. I just don't get why we don't win more games. As I finish cleaning up and packing my bag, Slim comes up and sets his bag beside mine.

"So how do you think we'll fare against Hillcrest this week?" he asks, not exuding the air of confidence I would hope to hear from one of our best players.

"I think we've got a fighting chance," I say, not looking him in the eye for fear he'll catch my doubt as well.

"What's our problem, Davis? We've got some great players and should be doing a lot better than we are."

I feel a little relieved that I'm not the only one worrying about how we can turn this season around. Slim has always been like that. We've played ball together since elementary school. We both love to win at anything we do, and we both lose sleep trying to figure out how we can make it happen.

"I'm not sure, Slim," I answer honestly. "I talked to Coach H. this morning, and he seems to think he's got the answer to our problem. I'm not sure what it is yet, but I figure, if he can pull off a state championship with the baseball team, then maybe he knows what we're doing wrong. Heck, his baseball team didn't have half the talent we've got, and they rolled through state like it was a day at the park."

"I hope you're right," Slim says. "But it's gotta happen fast. We've only got a few games to go before we won't even have a chance to play in districts."

"Yeah, I know. Don't remind me."

If we lose to Hillcrest and then lose one more game, it would take a miracle to get us to the playoffs. Not that I'm already counting the Hillcrest game as a loss, but I'm not sure how we'll pull it off.

"I better get going," I say as I jam the last few things in my bag and make my way out of the locker room.

Feeling the weight of the team on my shoulders, I stare at my shoes as I walk out into the hall and smack-dab into—of all people—Samantha Wilmington, knocking the book she was carrying to the floor and sending her for a spin.

I fumble around, trying to pick up her book and maintain my composure. If I ever thought I had a chance, I'm sure I just blew it.

"I'm sorry," I stammer.

"Oh, it's okay, Andy," she says as she straightens out a few of the pages that were smashed as the book hit the floor.

No one calls me Andy but my family, but I guess this corrects my prior belief that Samantha doesn't know me from Adam.

"Are you okay?" I ask as I feel my face turn bright red; I search the scene for a rock to hide under.

"I'm fine. Don't worry about it," she assures me. "I was watching you guys finish up your practice. I hope your game this week against Hillcrest goes well."

In addition to being a brainiac, Samantha also plays on the girl's basketball team and is a pretty good ball player. Their practice usually gets out a little before ours.

"Thanks," I say nervously. "I hope we can pull it off."

"You don't sound too confident," she says, catching the doubt in my voice.

"Oh, I think we can beat 'em. We've just had a couple of rough games lately and need to pull it together."

"Well, good luck. I better get going," she says and makes her way toward the parking lot.

Here goes nothing.

"Can I walk you out to your car?" No doubt that, after knocking a girl down, I'm going out on a limb, but she does at least know my name, so that's got to be worth something.

"Sure." She smiles as I offer to take her bag and throw it over my shoulder.

"What do you have in here?" I blurt out before I think the comment all the way through. I wouldn't have asked, but her bag weighs a ton.

"Just schoolbooks and my gym clothes." She seems a little embarrassed, and I wish I hadn't said anything. Trying quickly to change the subject, I ask another dumb question.

"So, how did you get so good at math?"

Clearly, I'm no romancer. Knock a girl down, question the contents of her bag, and then ask her about math. I'm a loser—it's clear.

"I don't know." She doesn't seem fazed by my obvious lack of social skills. "I guess I've always just enjoyed the way math brings together a lot of abstract ideas and makes solving problems much easier. It just makes sense to me."

"Have you been talking to Coach Hunter as well?"

"What do you mean?" She seems confused.

"Oh, never mind. I was just talking to him this morning, and he was telling me the same thing. Saying how math—or algebra—is the answer to all of my problems. I just wondered if he had told you the same thing."

"No, I haven't talked with him about that. I think he could be right though. It's fun once you get the hang of it."

With that we are at her car—a nice, new Honda Accord. I'll have to wait until she's driven off to hop into the old El Camino.

The Profit Equation

"Well, thank you for carrying my bag, Andy."

I almost look around to see who she's calling Andy. It's still a little weird, but I'm sure I could get used to her calling me anything she wants to.

"No problem, and sorry again for running you down in the hallway."

I hand her the bag and watch as she drives out of the parking lot.

Samantha Wilmington, I think to myself. *She knows who I am, and she actually likes math. Wow!* Two things I could hardly have imagined possible.

Chapter 5

Wednesday flies by, unlike most school days. It all starts when Samantha says hi to me in the hall. Maybe my luck is finally changing for the better.

English, auto body, and PE go by quickly as I look forward to algebra—another chance to see Samantha and an opportunity to try and figure out this whole algebra thing again.

Coach starts class by reviewing order of operations one last time.

"Remember guys, parentheses first, then multiplication and division, and finally left to right."

He writes it on the board.
1. Parentheses
2. Multiplication and Division
3. Left to Right

I think I can handle that.

"Now let's move on to solving for unknown variables," Coach begins.

"There will be times when the equation you have is close to what you need, but the letters and numbers are in the wrong order." He starts to write an equation on the board. "Let's say we have this equation." He points to the equation.

$A + B = 5$

"If we know that A equals 3, we need to figure out what B equals. The first thing that you have to do is isolate the variable you are trying to solve for. You do this by moving everything but the unknown variable to the right-hand side of the equation. In this example, you can subtract A from both sides, and you will leave B alone on the left like this."

$$\cancel{A} + B - \cancel{A} = 5 - A$$

"Then,"

$$B = 5 - A$$

"Then,"

$$B = 5 - 3$$

"Then,"

$$B = 2$$

"Once you get the hang of it, you'll be able to do it in your sleep," Coach says confidently.

This seems easy enough, but I'm sure Coach is just going easy on us for starters. Sure enough, the next equation is tougher.

"Let's try another one."

Coach looks pretty excited as he starts to write another equation on the board. "This time let's use multiplication and division as well as addition and subtraction. Here's the equation."

$$\frac{A}{B} + 3 = C$$

"Let's say that B equals 4 and C equals 5. Try and solve for A this time."

I don't even know where to start, I think to myself.

"Okay, lets start the same way we did last time, by subtracting 3 from both sides to move the 3 over to the right."

$$\frac{A}{B} + \cancel{3} - \cancel{3} = C - 3$$

"Then,"

$$\frac{A}{B} = C - 3$$

"Now we need to get *A* alone. We need to get *B* off the bottom of the equation, so let's multiply both sides of the equation by *B* like this."

$$\frac{A}{B} \times B = (C - 3) \times B$$

"When you have a variable on the bottom of an equation and then multiply it on the top of an equation you can cross them off like this."

$$\frac{A}{\cancel{B}} \times \cancel{B} = (C - 3) \times B$$

"Now we have …"

$$A = (C - 3) \times B$$

"So if *B* equals 4 and *C* equals 5, we have:"

$$A = (5 - 3) \times 4$$

"Now we follow our order of operations—parentheses and then multiplication, like this:

$$A = (2) \times 4$$

"Then,"

$A = 8$

"Really not too bad." Coach grins. "I even think it's fun. Nothing like having a problem and solving it."

I have to admit it is interesting to watch Coach solve the problems. I don't know if I'd go as far as to say it's fun, but I'll give him interesting.

We go on and work a few more problems on the board before class is over. By the end of class, I feel okay about this "solving for the unknown variable" thing. With a little more practice, I could maybe even do it on my own.

When the bell rings and class is over, Coach catches me at the door. Samantha happens to be right behind me and overhears our conversation.

"We still on for tomorrow morning, Davis?"

"Sure thing, Coach. I'll be here. I'm curious now to see how you can apply all this problem solving to some real-life problems."

"It'll take some time, Davis." Coach is clearly trying to make sure I walk before I run.

Unfortunately, I don't have a lot of time to spare before I'll be jobless and the captain of a basketball team that is out of the running for the state championship. I hope that whatever he has up his sleeve will help quickly.

As I head down the hall for Spanish, Samantha catches up to me.

"So you're meeting with Coach H. in the morning? Mind if I tag along? I'm interested to hear what he's telling you ... you know, seeing how we both think math is fun and all." She looks pretty excited. I don't know how excited I am to have Samantha along as I try to figure out all of my problems, but I don't have the heart to tell her no.

"Sure, why not? Maybe you can translate for me when he starts talking his crazy math language."

Chapter 6

As the last bell of the day rings, I head for the gym. I'm in for a long night. After practice, I've got to book it to work. I close tonight at the store, and I'm curious to see what happened with the DM yesterday.

But first: basketball practice. We've got our big game tomorrow night, so we'll have our regular pregame practice—drills and scrimmaging—and then we'll talk strategy of sorts.

Slim is waiting for me in the locker room when I show up.

"Did you figure out what we need to do differently yet?" He's chomping at the bit to see if I've got the golden answer to turning our team around. I hate to disappoint him.

"No, not yet. I don't talk to Coach H. again until tomorrow morning, but I'm guessing that this solution he has in mind may not work quite as quickly as we need it to."

"Didn't you tell him we don't have much time? If we can't start winning soon, we're done."

"I know, I know. I'll tell Coach in the morning that if he could work his magic sooner than later, we'd really appreciate it."

"We better hustle before we're late for practice. I don't want to run."

That's one of Wally's crazy rules. For each minute you're late, you run a lap. It's not one of my favorite rules, but it does make sure the guys are on time to practice.

As we start practice, Wally calls me over.

"How ya feeling, Davis? Ready for the game tomorrow?" Wally's all business. He loves basketball and enjoys working with us on improving our game.

"I'm doing well. Hoping everybody brings their *A* game tomorrow. I think we have a good shot, if we can play well together." I can't tell him that it's going to take a miracle to win this game.

"I've been looking back over your field goal percentage for the last couple of games, and it keeps getting better." Wally is rummaging through his notebook, looking for something. "Here we are. The first game of the season, you made 47 percent of your shots. Since then, you've shot 49 percent, 53 percent, 50 percent, and last week against Skyline, you put up 62 percent. Just wanted to tell you great job and keep up the good work. The team average is following your lead as well. Let's keep moving in the right direction."

"Thanks, Coach." I bite my tongue, but I want to ask, "Why then is the team losing so many games?" If our field goal percentage, which is Wally's statistic of choice, keeps improving, then we ought to be winning more games.

I rejoin the team as we finish up the passing drill.

"What did Wally want?" Charley asks as he catches his breath.

"Just to say that our field goal percentage is on the rise. He watches that thing like a hawk." It's true. I almost wonder if he watches our field goal percentage more closely than our win-loss record. Pick your passion, I guess.

Wally interrupts our conversation with the blow of his whistle.

"Alright guys, let's break up for scrimmages."

We scrimmage hard for a half hour, and then Wally calls us all to the bleachers to talk strategy. I don't know if I'd really call it strategy. It's usually the same old, "work the ball around until you have an open shot" talk. Wally hates missed shots more than anything—probably rightfully so. Most of the guys have become a little gun shy, because of all the focus on taking high-percentage shots. I can't say that I think it's a bad strategy. Logic would have it that if you make a greater percentage of shots you'd win more games. It just doesn't seem to be working out that way for us.

Wally outlines a couple of plays on the whiteboard, and then we start talking about matchups. We play zone on defense unless we get too far behind, and then we switch up and play man defense to try to close down whoever seems to be on fire.

Wally talks through each of our positions and who we will likely match up against. Hillcrest has a good team, and all of our guys will have to step up if we're going to win this game. They have a lot of players who could have a breakout game and run up their score.

When we're done strategizing, I run back to the locker room and shower quickly, so I can get to work on time. In the shower, I can't help but smile at the irony—at work, my stats stink, and things aren't going well; on the court, my stats are great, and things aren't going well. It just doesn't make sense.

Jimmy's waiting for me when I show up to work.

"Hey, Davis. Clock in, and then we need to talk a bit."

I guess he's going right for the jugular.

I clock into the computer and follow Jimmy to the backroom.

"So how was the visit from the DM?" I might as well lay it on the table, since there's no hope of dodging the bullet.

"He liked what we'd done with the store." Jimmy tries to smile. "But he said that the home office was really ramping up the emphasis on stats again, not that it was ever really ramped down."

No kidding, I think to myself. Since the day I started, it's been stats, stats, and more stats.

"Anyway," Jimmy continues, now looking at his shoes, "the long and the short of it is that, since sales have been slipping lately in the store, the pressure is on for everyone whose stats are below average to get 'em up or get out. We have a month to get our stats up. If we can't get our sales up—by improving everyone's stats—we all may be looking for new jobs."

The Profit Equation

Now that's something I didn't expect to hear from Jimmy—talk of him having to look for a new job as well. His stats have always been great. I guess that, as the manager of the store, he's got to make sure everyone is up to par. I don't really know what to say.

Jimmy goes on before I think of anything intelligent to offer up.

"You're pulling us down, Davis. I think you're a hard worker—no question there—but your stats are way off the store average. I'd love to keep you around, but if we really have to turn our stats around, I can't be carrying any dead weight."

"So, I'm done? No warning? Nothing?" I ask in disbelief.

"I wish we had more time, Davis. I really do. I'm willing to give you a couple more weeks, but only on the condition that you can make some improvements in a hurry."

I feel a little relieved but not much.

"So tell me what I need to do. I'll do whatever I can to keep my job." I feel desperate.

"The company's *Average Sale* is $52.00, and the company's average *Items per Transaction* is 2.5. Our store's stats are at $49.00 and 2.0. Right now, you're sitting at $42.00 and 1.8. I need you to at least be at the store average within two weeks …" He doesn't finish his sentence, but I can fill in the blank.

"Okay, so I need to bring my *Average Sale* up to $49.00 and my *Items per Transaction* to 2.0. I'll give it my best."

Unfortunately, it's not like I've been sitting around doing nothing. I hope he doesn't think that I can hustle a little harder and, all of a sudden, my stats will miraculously improve. I've honestly been giving everything I have. The last thing I want is to lose my job. I guess I'll have to find a way to get better. It sounds like my only option.

Chapter 7

I wake up Thursday before the alarm goes off. I hardly slept a wink. Between the big game tonight and the ultimatum at work, I had a thousand thoughts racing through my mind all night.

I hurry to school and even beat Coach H. there. When he shows up, he must be able to tell I had a rough night.

"Davis, you look like death warmed over. You okay?" He looks concerned. I like Coach H. Despite the fact that he teaches algebra, he's a great teacher and really is concerned about all of his students. That's a lot more than I can say about most of my teachers. It seems like most of them can't stand us.

"I'm okay, Coach. Big game tonight, you know. Just a case of the butterflies. That, and I've got two weeks to get my stats up at work, or I'm done."

"Sounds like time is of the essence then. Let's get started. By the way, I ran into Samantha last night after school, and she said she was joining us this morning." He gives me a wink.

I ignore his wink and move on, "So, Coach. Do you really think this stuff can help? I don't have much time at work or with the team. Can it really work that fast?"

"Sure it can, Davis. You've got to do it right though, so you'll have to be a little patient, but I think we can turn things around pretty quickly."

"So, what's the first thing we need to do? Do you have some equation I need to memorize? Is the secret in my book somewhere?"

The Profit Equation

At that, Samantha pokes her head in the door. "Sorry I'm late, Coach. Hi, Andy."

Coach pulls up a chair for her. "No problem. How are you this morning, Samantha?"

"I'm doing well, thanks." Samantha smiles at me.

"Well, you're just in time, Samantha. We were about ready to unlock the secrets of the universe and solve all of Davis' problems."

"Ha, ha." I pretend to laugh. How embarrassing. Now Samantha probably thinks I'm a dork who runs girls down in the hallway, has no social skills, and is a basket case of problems who's seeking counseling from the algebra teacher.

Coach continues, "All kidding aside, this morning, I'm going to start teaching you a process that will change the way you view problems the rest of your life. If you can stick this out, you will begin to see them more as opportunities than as problems.

"Let's start at the beginning. Samantha, last time I was telling Davis how algebra is kind of like a puzzle. It's a process that takes a lot of broken parts, the puzzle pieces, and restores them to a complete picture. Remember that Davis, restoration of broken parts?"

"Yeah, I remember."

"Samantha," Coach continues, "if you were going to do a puzzle—any kind of puzzle—what is the first thing you would need?"

"I don't know." Samantha thinks for a minute. "Maybe an idea of what the puzzle was supposed to look like when I was finished."

"That's right." Coach grins. "You think about any puzzle you've ever done. At some point before the problem is solved, you have to have a clear picture in your mind of what the solution looks like."

I think of the mint condition Mustang poster hanging on the wall in the auto body shop. It really does make the project easier and much more worthwhile; we can see the end from the beginning.

"You've both heard the story of Alice in Wonderland, right?" Coach asks.

We nod.

"Do you remember what happened when Alice met the Cheshire cat?"

I answer this one; it may be the only answer I'll know.

"Sure, Alice came to a fork in the road and asked the Cheshire cat which road she ought to take. The cat answered her by asking where she wanted to go. Alice said she really didn't know. To that, the cat responded that it really didn't matter then what road she took."

"That's right, Davis." Coach is on a roll now. "If you don't know what you are trying to accomplish, you'll never get there."

Coach literally jumps from his chair and heads to the board. As he continues to talk, he starts to write, "The fact that you need to know where you are going applies to both real-life problems and algebra. Let's look at an equation, and I'll show you what I mean."

He's written on the board:

$$A + B \times C$$

$$A = 4$$
$$B = 2$$

"Samantha, why don't you tell me what the letter C equals?" Coach asks.

"Well," Samantha begins and then stops. "I don't think I can, can I?"

"No, you can't." Coach goes back to the board. "Without an equals sign, you don't have a complete equation. At the heart of every equation is an equals sign. This is what allows you to solve the problem. The equals sign drives your equation.

"You see, in algebra and life, until you can identify what you are trying to solve for and insert an equals sign in the equation, all of the broken parts will remain just that—broken parts.

"If I were to change the equation to look like this …"

$$A + B \times C = 6$$

"Now you could solve it, right?" Coach hands the chalk to Samantha. She walks to the board and goes to work.

$$4 + 2 \times C = 6$$

$$\cancel{4} + 2 \times C - \cancel{4} = 6 - 4$$

$$2 \times C = 2$$

$$\frac{\cancel{2} \times C}{\cancel{2}} = \frac{2}{2}$$

$$C = 1$$

"Great work, Samantha." Coach says as she hands him back the chalk.

"So, how can we apply this to a real-life problem?" I ask, trying to refocus Coach on the fact that letters and numbers won't do much for me until I know how to apply it in real life.

"Good question, Davis." Coach walks back to the board. "The first thing you have to do is try to figure out what the answer to your problem equals.

"Let's set up a simple equation."

$$\text{Success} = X$$

"The first thing we have to establish is what does *Success* equal. For every problem, the answer will be different. But for every problem, there is an answer. For the process I want to teach you, if you can start by defining *Success* in terms of a single number, then you have won half the battle; you have in your mind that picture of what all of the broken parts look like when they are restored.

"Let's take an example of running a race." Coach gets up again and writes on the board. "Let's say that your goal is to a run a race in 40 minutes flat. In this case, your equation looks like this."

Success = 40 minutes

"If you wanted to save $400 to buy a new pair of skis, your equation would look like this."

Success = $400

"The first step is as simple as that. Define the solution to your problem—or your success—as a single number."

At that, the first bell rings, and our time is up. I think I see what I need to do next. Figure out a way to define the solution in terms of a single number.

As we pack up and walk out the door, Coach calls after us, "Remember, for this to work, you have to think big. Try to define success in the broadest sense first. For starters, just pick one problem, and then once you get the hang of it, you can apply the concept to any of your problems. Come back on Monday, and we'll see what you've figured out."

Chapter 8

"So, what do you think?" I ask Samantha as we walk down the hall toward our first class.

Samantha smiles. "It'll be fun. I like Coach H., and I'm interested to see where he's going with this. So, where do you think you'll start?"

"I was thinking I'd start with this problem I have at work. My boss is all over me about these statistics we measure, and I'm having a hard time improving them. Hopefully, Coach can help me figure out how to get things turned around. What about you? I'm sure a girl like you doesn't have many problems."

"Are you kidding? I was walking down the hall last night and this guy nearly ran me down and wrinkled some of the pages in the book I was reading."

Samantha winks at me as I feel my face turn bright red again. How embarrassing.

"I'm just teasing you. I have plenty of problems, but maybe we should start with your work problem and then, like Coach said, we can apply this process of his to our other problems." Samantha turns to go into the chemistry room.

"See ya in algebra," I call after her.

As I sit down in English, I run back through our meeting with Coach. You have to see the whole picture in order to solve the puzzle. Alice in Wonderland had to know where she was going before she could know which road to take. There has to be an equals sign in an equation before you can solve the problem.

"Davis, I was hoping you could read something for us, but I'm not sure you're with us today." Mrs. Anderson, my English teacher, interrupts my thoughts.

"Sorry, Mrs. Anderson," I stammer.

"Okay, class. Today, we are reading from the writings of Elbert Hubbard. Hubbard was an American writer, publisher, artist, and philosopher who lived during the late 1800s and the early 1900s. He was most famous for his essay "Message to Garcia," but today we are going to read an excerpt from another of his works.

"Davis, if you would begin on page two seventy eight in our literature book with 'Keep your mind on …'"

"Yes, ma'am." I flip through my book until I find the page. "Here we go: 'Keep your mind on the great and splendid thing you would like to do; and then, as the days go gliding by, you will find yourself unconsciously seizing the opportunities that are required for the fulfillment of your desire … Picture in your mind the able, earnest, useful person you desire to be, and the thought that you hold is hourly transforming you into that particular individual you so admire.'"[1]

"Thank you, Davis."

Mrs. Anderson calls on someone else to continue reading.

I look back at the passage I just read. I wonder if Coach H. talked to Mrs. Anderson and asked me to read that section today. It goes hand in hand with what Coach and I talked about this morning—identifying your goal and having a clear picture of what you want to accomplish. I'm sure the process Coach is planning to teach us will not leave our success to chance as much as the passage suggests, like "unconsciously seizing the opportunities." I am, however, confident that Coach would stand behind Mr. Hubbard in the philosophy of having a clear vision of what you want to accomplish as you embark on the journey of accomplishing it.

I start thinking about my trouble at work. If my issue was completely resolved, what would it look like? Well, I wouldn't be

---

[1] Elbert Hubbard, *Little Journeys to the Homes of the Great, Volume 5* (Project Gutenberg eBook, 2004), 131.

on a two-week tether that is on the verge of snapping, dropping me into unemployment. I would be at the top of the stats board and would be making more than minimum wage, because Jimmy couldn't afford to lose me.

So, success equals good stats. I wonder which of the stats I should pick: *Average Sale* or *IPT*. Coach said I could only pick one, so I'll have to figure out which is more important. I'd like to ask Jimmy on Saturday when I work, but I'm sure his answer will be that I have to improve both.

Maybe it doesn't really matter which one I pick. In theory, if I sell more items, I ought to have a better *Average Sale*.

I'll have to keep thinking about this later, because I have to get back to English. Mrs. Anderson is a stickler about keeping up in the readings, and I'm already a few pages behind. The last thing I need is to fail another class.

We finish reading Hubbard's writings and Mrs. Anderson gives us our next assignment. While I'm pretty good at English, I'm not sure what some of these guys were thinking when they wrote their books.

I'm anxious to go to algebra today and learn more about solving for variables. I think Coach said we were going to be working on that for a few more days.

When algebra finally rolls around, I hurry to class so I can sit close enough to make sure I catch everything that is going on.

Coach picks up where we left off in the last class.

"Today, we are going to continue solving for variables but take it a little bit further. Often when you need to solve an equation, you won't be given the actual equation. You will have a problem explained to you, and then you have to create the equation before you can solve it. They call this a word problem. Let's try one."

Coach opens up his book and reads a problem.

"John fills up his car at the gas station before going on a short trip. The odometer in John's car is broken. John knows that he gets 20 miles per gallon of gas. When he gets to where he is

Michael D. Batt

going he fills his car back up and pays $7.50 for 3.2 gallons of gas. How far did John drive?

"Okay, the first thing we want to do is identify the variables that we know ..."

Miles per gallon = 20
Gallons of gas used = 3.2
Cost for 3.2 gallons = $7.50

" ... and the variable that we don't know."

Miles driven

"Now, we are ready to build the equation. It looks like this."

$$\frac{\text{Miles driven}}{3.2 \text{ gallons used}} = \frac{20 \text{ miles}}{1 \text{ gallon used}}$$

"Davis, do you want to come up and solve for *Miles Driven* now?" Coach asks as he holds out the chalk.

"Sure, I'll give it a try, but I have a question first. What about the cost for the 3.2 gallons of gas? Why didn't we use that variable?" I stand up and take the chalk but wait for the answer.

"That's a great question, Davis." Coach grins. "This happens all of the time in algebra. You have variables that are good variables but aren't really applicable to the equation that you are trying to solve. Sometimes, the hardest part is trying to weed out the variables that apply and those that don't. In this case, the *Cost per Gallon* is a true variable but we don't need it to find out how far he drove."

I can buy that, I think. I turn to the board to try to solve the problem. I think back to how we solved the last problem and remember that, to get a variable off the bottom of an equation, I have to multiply the top of the equation on both sides by that variable. Coach also tells me as I start to write that, for a problem like this when you have the same units on the top and the bottom, you can cross them off as well. I write on the board.

$$\frac{\text{Miles driven}}{\cancel{3.2 \text{ gallons used}}} \times \cancel{3.2 \text{ gallons used}} = \frac{20 \text{ miles}}{1 \cancel{\text{ gallon used}}} \times 3.2 \cancel{\text{ gallons used}}$$

Miles driven = 20 miles x 3.2

Miles driven = 64 miles

"Great job, Davis."
I hand the chalk to Coach and sit down.
It's starting to come together, slowly. Up to now, we have just been solving for As and Bs. Now that we have a real-life problem that we've worked through, I can see how this might be useful. I don't know that I could build the equation on my own, but I trust that Coach can get me there.
For now, I guess I just need to work on getting the solutions to my problem stated as a single number. Then I can worry about building equations and solving for variables.

Michael D. Batt

CHAPTER 9

As the ref tosses the ball into the air, Charley stretches and tips the ball into the backcourt where Slim grabs it and passes it down the court to me.
We play patient ball, moving the ball around and looking for an open shot. I pass the ball over to Bill, who sends it inside to Jeff, who kicks it back out to me. I fake a pass to Charley and cut for the center of the key where I pull up for a ten-foot jumper. Nothing but net!
That's the way to start a game. I hope we can keep it up. At the other end of the court, Hillcrest works the ball inside to their big man, who puts up a bank. It comes off long, and I dive for the ball. "Foul! With the body. Number 11."

I look at my jersey in disbelief. There was no way I fouled that guy. I run over to the ref and try to plead my case, even though I know it's pointless. In the history of basketball, there has probably never been a ref who reversed a call like that. Anyway, I've got to try.
Hillcrest gets the ball at midcourt and pushes it inside for an easy basket. Wally is up now and pacing. He hates it when we give up easy shots. At the other end of the court, we push it inside, and Slim answers with a bank shot.

Two minutes into the first quarter, I get my second foul. It was a stupid foul; I tried to reach around their point guard as he dribbled down the sideline.

Wally calls a timeout and puts me on the bench. *Great, just what we need.* It's the first quarter, and I'm already in foul trouble. We're doomed.

As I sit at the far end of the bench, knowing I won't be back in until the second quarter—at the earliest—I start to think again about my conversation with Coach this morning and my goal to identify my problems in terms of a single number.

I'm sure Wally would tell me that my goal ought to be field-goal percentage. He preaches it every chance he has. Right now, my field goal percentage is 100 percent; you can't get much better than that. Maybe I could pretend I was sick and sit out the rest of the game. I'd have a perfect field goal percentage for the first time ever!

Obviously, that can't be right. How can I succeed at accomplishing my goal and let my team fail? Somehow this thought makes my goal seem out of line. But how can I control the outcome of the rest of the team? Granted, I am the point guard and I control who gets the ball to some extent. From there though, they can make the choice to shoot a poor shot, or they may throw a bad pass that results in a turnover.

I think back to Coach's last comment to Samantha and me as we left class this morning. "Remember, for this to work you have to think big. Try to define success in the broadest sense first." Laying aside the fact that I don't know how I can control the outcome, let's think big.

Thinking big, success has to equal winning the game—no question. I can't think of any other result that could be defined as success if I'm thinking beyond my own performance.

Now how can I state that as a number? It clearly can't be a statistic for an individual or probably even a statistic for the team. When I was taken out of the game, as a team we had only shot two shots, and we had made both of them. If we were to say that success for the team was defined as a certain shooting percentage, we should stop shooting altogether—we are perfect right now. No, shooting percentage can't be it. Maybe we could define success as a certain number of points that we score in the game.

Michael D. Batt

Looking up to the scoreboard as I mull this over in my head, I'm surprised to find that we're keeping it close. We are only down by one with twenty seconds left in the quarter. The score is 14–13.

We take possession on a turnover and move down the court for the last shot of the quarter. Bill, who took over at point when I was taken out, moves the ball around the perimeter, looking for an open man and eating up some time. With six seconds left on the clock, he rifles a pass underneath to Jeff, who drives to the hoop. Jeff fakes a shot and then scoops the ball up and under for a reverse just as the buzzer goes off.

We huddle at the bench; we're now up 15–14.

My mind is racing. Say our goal is a number of points. Let's say that, since we are at 15 in the first quarter, that our goal for the game is 60 points. That's a single number that would probably equal success—assuming, of course, that we can hold Hillcrest to no more than 59 points.

As we break the huddle, Wally tells me that I'm back in the game.

As we walk out onto the court, I catch up with Slim.

"Hey, Slim. If we can score 60 points tonight, I'll buy you dinner after the game."

Slim looks at me like I'm crazy, but he agrees; he's never one to pass up a free meal.

By the half, we're just over halfway to the 60-point mark at 31. We head to the locker room ahead by 4.

I think of the quote I read this morning in English: "Keep your mind on the great and splendid thing you would like to do; and then, as the days go gliding by, you will find yourself unconsciously seizing the opportunities that are required for the fulfillment of your desire." In this case, it may be minutes instead of days, and I can't say that the goal Slim and I set is making all the difference, but it has clearly driven us to push the ball more quickly and look for shots faster, knowing that we need enough time to get the rest of our points in for the quarter.

The Profit Equation

I'm not sure what else Coach H. has in mind for this process of defining success as a number, but I can definitely see the value—even after just the first half—in having a concrete number that we are shooting for.

Wally gives us a little pep talk in the locker room and tells us how well we're doing.

I whisper to Slim, "Only 29 more points. Can you taste the onion rings yet?"

We bust our tails during the second half, and by some stroke of fate, when the final buzzer sounds, the scoreboard reads 62–58.

We did it.

On top of this being a huge victory, I have bought myself a little more time to learn the rest of this problem-solving process that Coach H. is trying to teach me.

While the clear, concise goal made a distinct difference in our performance tonight, I'm not positive we could duplicate it by setting another goal of 60 points. There must be something more that Coach has in mind. Now that I have a better picture in my mind of what the final puzzle looks like—at least for the basketball team—I need to learn the process of putting the pieces together on a consistent basis, so we can repeat our performance during the next game.

Tonight though, it was victory, and I owe Slim dinner at Molly's.

"Hey, Davis." Slim smacks me on the back in the locker room. "We did it! Can you believe it? We actually did it."

"Yeah, you played your heart out, man. Great job!" I look around the locker room and see all the guys in great spirits. *This is what it should be like*, I think to myself. *We've got the talent. We ought to play like this every night.*

"We still on for dinner at Molly's?" Slim grins from ear to ear.

Chapter 10

I wake up earlier than usual on Friday morning and tiptoe through the frost on the front lawn to grab the morning paper. I'm interested in seeing the stats from our game last night. I rip the sports section out and leave the rest on the kitchen table. I head to my room. As I suspected, Slim led the way in scoring with a dominant 18 points—over a quarter of our total.

My game was so-so, but I'll take a win any day, even if it means I have slightly lower stats—that is, as long as Wally lets me continue to play the minutes. After I scan everyone's individual stats, I read through the team's stats. Field goal percentage for the team was 38 percent. Not too great!

I skip ahead to Hillcrest's box scores. They shot 40 percent. Interesting. We had a lower shooting percentage, but we scored more points.

After reviewing the rest of the stats and reading the article about the game, I hustle and get ready for school.

My morning classes drag as I wait for algebra. Samantha caught me in the hall before school started and congratulated me on our win last night. The girls play tonight, and I plan on going to their game as well.

Finally, algebra rolls around. As I come into class, Coach H. meets me at the door.

"Great game last night, Davis. Looks like you figured out what success was for the team."

"Well, I figured out that it wasn't shooting percentage." I feel proud that I made it at least that far. "We set a goal to score 60 points, and that worked out pretty well. Hillcrest had a better shooting percentage, but we still beat them." I pause to see if Coach has any thoughts, but he just nods, so I continue, "Obviously, there has to be more than just setting a goal. When can you teach us the next steps? I don't know if I can wait until Monday."

I hate to sound anxious, but I guess I am.

"Easy, Davis. Rome wasn't built in a day. Before we can go on, I want to make sure you have mastered this first step: defining success or your goal as a single number. Once you have that down, then we will move on to the next part."

"Fair enough, Coach."

There's no point in arguing. It's true that I still need to think some more about my stats at work. After the game last night, I'm not so sure *Average Sale* or *IPT* is the number for my goal at work. If an individual stat doesn't cut it in basketball, I don't know that it will be the answer at work either.

I sit down next to Samantha and see that she is busy working on something in her notebook.

"Hey, Samantha."

"Hi, Andy. How's your day been?"

"Pretty good," I say, and that's no lie. Coming off a victory against Hillcrest, how could it be anything but great?

"How is your goal-setting going?" she asks. "Any luck yet?"

"I'm still working on it. I think I learned a few things last night in the basketball game. Going into the game, I thought shooting percentage was the end-all—or at least, that is what Wally would have led me to believe. As we played, I realized that I could come out of the game shooting 100 percent, and we could still lose the game."

Samantha nods in understanding, so I continue.

"As I thought about my work, I realized that some of the stats we measure there might not be the right goals either. Before last night, I was pretty confident that the answer would be *Average Sale* or *Items per Transaction*. Now I'm not so sure. I need to think about it a little more."

"I'm sure you'll figure it out."

"Hopefully so," I say. I don't feel too confident yet.

Coach is getting class started.

"So who can tell us what we've learned so far?" Coach asks. "Davis, how 'bout you give it a shot?"

"Okay, Coach. Why not? We've talked about order of operations, solving for variables, and …" My mind draws a blank.

Coach seems satisfied that I remembered at least a couple of things. "Remember last time? The problem about figuring out how far the man had driven?"

"Oh, yeah," I say. "We started talking about setting up equations when we have a problem that is only expressed in words."

"That's right," Coach says. "As a matter of fact, probably the only place you'll ever be given a clear-cut equation and variables will be right here within these four walls. Everywhere else you go, someone will explain a problem in words, and then you'll have to figure out how to set it up. Let's spend a little more time working on building equations." Coach walks over to the board.

"Today, let's work on a classic algebra problem. Here it is: If Jen is 3 years older than Tom, who is 5 years older than Anne, who is twice as old as Larry, who is 6, then how old is Jen?

"Sometimes a problem will take multiple equations in order to get to the final answer. Let's start by setting up a couple of different equations, and then we will work on combining them."

Jen = Tom + 3 years

"Remember that it is critical to write the units of measurement as you go along. In this case, *years* is the unit of measurement."

Tom = Anne + 5 years

Anne = Larry × 2 years

Larry = 6 years

The Profit Equation

"Now there are two ways to do this. We could figure out the ages of each of the individuals separately or we could just build one equation that tells us Jen's age. Let's try that for fun. The first step is to combine the first two equations. We can do this by substituting what we know about Tom into the first equation like this."

$$\text{Jen} = (\text{Anne} + 5 \text{ years}) + 3 \text{ years}$$

"We will put parenthesis around it for now to note that when we start to calculate we need to calculate this first. The next step is to take what we know about Anne and insert it into the equation like this."

$$\text{Jen} = ((\text{Larry} \times 2 \text{ years}) + 5 \text{ years}) + 3 \text{ years}$$

"When you have two sets of parentheses, you always start from the innermost set and work outward. Finally, we need to input what we know about Larry into this equation."

$$\text{Jen} = ((6 \text{ years} \times 2 \text{ years}) + 5 \text{ years}) + 3 \text{ years}$$

"So:"

$$\text{Jen} = 20 \text{ years}$$

"This skill of substituting information into equations for unknown variables will come in handy as you begin to work with more complicated equations." Coach leans back against the board. "You'll find, more often than not, that you may not have exactly the data that you are looking for, but if you can build two or three equations and then begin substituting or combining them, you can eventually create an equation where there is only one unknown variable. That is the key: getting every equation down to one unknown variable. Once you do this, then you can solve for that unknown variable.

Michael D. Batt

"We do this all the time in real life without even thinking about it," Coach continues. "Let's try one more problem, and I'll show you what I mean. Here is the problem: You want to go to lunch today. You know that you have $30 in your wallet. You also know that, if you are going to make it to work today, you need to put some gas in your car. Your car gets 15 miles to the gallon, and you need to drive 20 miles to get to work and home. You also plan on going on a date tonight and will need to drive another 20 miles to pick up your date. So in all, you better plan on driving 50 miles so you have enough to get to the next gas station. Gas costs $2.50 a gallon. You are planning on taking your date for ice cream, which will cost you $10.00, and then to rent a movie, which will cost you $5.00. Lunch would cost you $5.00. Do you have enough money to go to lunch?"

This should be cake. I've gone through this kind of logic in my head a thousand times. I've never thought that I was actually using algebra to figure it out though.

"Let's write down what we know." Coach has erased the last problem from the board and is ready to go again.

Current Cash = $30

$$\text{Cost of Gas per Gallon} = \frac{\$2.50}{1 \text{ Gallon}}$$

$$\text{Gallons of Gas per Miles Driven} = \frac{1 \text{ Gallon}}{15 \text{ Miles Driven}}$$

Distance You Need to Drive = 50 miles

Cost of Date = $15

Cost of Lunch = $5

"Now let's write the equation, trying to figure out how much we have to spend on lunch. We can then compare that to the $5.00 amount and see if we have enough."

The Profit Equation

Amount Available for Lunch = Current Cash − Cost of Date − Cost of Gas

"We know what *Current Cash* is, and we know what *Cost of Date* is but we don't know right offhand what *Cost of Gas* is, so let's make a second equation."

$$\text{Cost of Gas} = \text{Distance You Need to Drive} \times \frac{\text{Gallons of Gas}}{\text{Miles Driven}} \times \frac{\text{Cost of Gas}}{\text{Gallons of Gas}}$$

"Now we can input the variables we know into the second equation to find out the *Cost of Gas*. Let's do that, and then we can stick this number into the first equation to see if you have enough for lunch."

$$\text{Cost of Gas} = 50 \text{ Miles} \times \frac{1 \text{ Gallon}}{15 \text{ Miles}} \times \frac{\$2.50}{1 \text{ Gallon}}$$

"Since we have like units we can cross off the similar units and then do the multiplication. When you are done all that will be left is the dollar signs, which is the unit of measurement that you want for the cost of the gas.

$$\text{Cost of Gas} = 50 \; \cancel{\text{Miles}} \times \frac{1 \; \cancel{\text{Gallon}}}{15 \; \cancel{\text{Miles}}} \times \frac{\$2.50}{1 \; \cancel{\text{Gallon}}}$$

"Then:"

Cost of Gas = $8.33

"If we stick this into the first equation, we have …"

Amount Available for Lunch = $30 − $15 − $8.33

"So:"

Amount Available for Lunch = $6.67

"You can go to lunch today." Coach smiles as he proves that this math stuff may actually have some real-life application. "You see, you already know how to do this. Now, it is just a matter of writing it down so you can solve for the unknown variable. Once you get the hang of it, you'll be solving all sorts of problems."

The rest of the day cruises by as I think back over the things we talked about in algebra. When I go to Samantha's game in the evening, I can't help but watch the game with my newfound understanding and appreciation of setting a goal and working toward it. They win the game by a long shot, and Samantha plays great!

CHAPTER 11

Saturday morning, I'm up and ready to go to work to see what I can figure out about this goal thing. I'm working a "burner" today—open to close. When I only work a few days a week, I sometimes end up working long hours on Saturdays.

When I show up, Jimmy is already there. He's been putting in some long hours himself these days.

"Hey, Davis," Jimmy greets me at the gate to the store. "You ready to make it happen today?"

"You bet," I say, forcing a smile. During my shift on Wednesday, I got lucky, and a lady came in to buy some presents for her grandkids. She went to town and, in one sale, shored up my stats for the night.

Today's a new day though, and the time bomb is still ticking to see if I can get my stats up to the store average. Despite the fact that I'm not sure if the stats we are working on are really the right answer, I know that my job depends on improving them. I've either got to get them up or figure out a way to bring Jimmy—and the DM—to see the error of their ways.

There are only three of us working today—Jimmy, Larry, and I—so we should be plenty busy. We hurry and count the tills and get the store tidied up a little before the gate goes up at ten o'clock.

As we work, I think to myself about our two stats—*Average Sale* and *Items per Transaction*. The store's *Average Sale* is $49.00 with an *IPT* of 2.0. That really shouldn't be too hard to get. We sell all sorts of sports stuff—jerseys, hats, T-shirts, mugs, key chains …

everything under the sun. With the sports fanatics who come through our doors, I shouldn't have any problem knocking down a $49.00 *Average Sale*—at least in theory. I've thought that before, but now that my job depends on it, I'll see what I can do.

At ten AM sharp, we roll up the gate to the store. The first hour is usually a little slow, but we have a few customers roll in when we open. In the morning, we usually get some mall walkers who are just finishing up their walks. They rarely buy anything, and if they do, it's not much.

Today is no exception. I walk up to an older gentleman and comment on his sweatshirt. "A Longhorns fan, huh? What did ya think of the game last Saturday?"

The man is in the mood to talk and gives me a play-by-play of the game. Finally when he has to take a break to breathe, I try to make the sale.

"We just got in the new Longhorn jackets this week. It's their best jacket yet."

I make my way over to the wall and pull a jacket down. He loves it. He tries it on over his sweatshirt and admires himself in the mirror. As he takes it off, he looks at the price tag and goes into "sticker shock."

"Seventy-five dollars for a jacket? Too rich for my blood." He can hardly believe it as he hands the jacket back to me.

"We do have a few less expensive items for the Longhorns," I say. I head over to the counter to pull out some of our miscellaneous items. I show him a key chain, a mug, and a shot glass—all with the Longhorn logo.

He looks at each of the items, and after taking his time to think it over, he says, "I've been needing a new key chain. I'll take it."

"Would you like a T-shirt or hat as well?" I ask.

"No, no. The key chain will do."

He pulls out his wallet and hands me three dollars.

Great! What a way to start the day. A $2.50 sale with only 1 item—I'm doomed. I ring up the key chain and put it in a bag for the man.

When he leaves the store, Jimmy comes over. "You're going to have to do better than that if you're going to hit the store average."

No kidding, I think to myself.

Larry comes over to offer his two bits as well. Larry's worked here for a couple of years, and next to Jimmy, he has the best stats in the store.

"Listen, Davis. If you want to get your stats up, you have to pick your customers. You know as well as I do that mall walkers will never go big. You have to target the people who look like they have money and are ready to spend."

It's true. Larry lies low until he sees some lady walk through the door with a rock on her finger that belongs in some museum, and then he goes in for the kill. He'll have the whole store laid out on the counter and will keep pushing until she's bought every item that we offer for her team … and her husband's and her son's. It's almost embarrassing how shameless he is, but he does have the stats to show that he knows how to work the system.

Jimmy isn't quite so obvious, but you can tell that, if some kid comes through the door with a bag of change, he'll be pretty hard-pressed to get any help from one of those two. Chances are I'll end up helping him, and then he'll walk out of the store like that old man with a key chain in tow. No wonder my stats stink.

I guess if I want to keep my job, I'll have to start playing the system a little more. I do have a hard time believing that our DM would want us to let sales walk out the door for the sake of saving our stats. But stats are the emphasis, so maybe they know something I don't.

The first hour creeps by without too many more customers. Around noon, Slim comes by to see what new Broncos merchandise we have. He's a huge Broncos fan and always gets the latest. We talk for a few minutes about the game Thursday night, and Jimmy tells him he read about his performance in the paper.

"All the credit goes to Davis here." Slim slaps me on the back. "He told me he'd take me to dinner down at Molly's diner if we could get to 60 points. We pulled together and made it happen."

"By the way, Davis," Slim says as he turns to me, "did you notice that our shooting percentage was worse than Hillcrest's, and we still pulled off the win? I could hardly believe it when I was looking at the stats yesterday."

"How does that work?" Jimmy asks. He graduated a few years ago and used to play for Wally. He was fully indoctrinated in the shooting percentage mentality as well. Maybe that's what makes him so worried about my stats here at the store.

"Simple really," I say. "I started thinking about it during the game. I came out of the game early in foul trouble and was one for one from the floor. I realized that I was shooting 100 percent. It hit me that it didn't really matter how well I shot—as a percentage anyway—as long as, when the final buzzer went off, we had put more points up on the board than the other team."

"The bottom line is," Slim says, grinning from ear to ear, "we beat Hillcrest, and that means we still have a shot at the tournament."

As a few more customers come in the store, Slim looks around a little and then says goodbye while we eye our new prospects, looking for the big spenders. I can't help but think that the lessons we learned on the court Thursday night have to have some application to what I'm trying to accomplish here at work. The question is how?

As I think back to the process I went through during the game to arrive at the 60 point goal, I realize that the first thing I did was ditch our time-proven stat in exchange for an overarching goal.

Jimmy says that *Average Sale* and *IPT* are the bread-and-butter of retail. If we were to ditch these stats in exchange for a loftier goal, what would it be? The obvious answer would be overall store sales. That is the one other thing that Jimmy seems to keep in the back of our minds as important. He's always quick to remind us, though, that, if we can drive the stats, the sales will fall into place. There isn't really any emphasis on sales—its stats, stats, and more stats.

When we have a break, I'll have to ask Jimmy what he thinks. There are a few customers over at the counter with a hat they'd like to purchase. Surprisingly, Larry is nowhere to be found. Jimmy is in the back of the store helping some other customers, who are loading up. I make my way to the counter and strike up a conversation with the kid and his girlfriend.

"So what brings you in today?" Maybe, if I'm lucky, I can get them to buy another hat or a T-shirt.

"Not much," the kid says. "Just need to pick up this hat."

"Could I interest you in another hat? We have a special this month. Buy one, get the second half off."

"No thanks. This is all we need." He seems to be in a hurry to get out of here.

"How 'bout a key chain or mug?"

"All I need is the hat today, okay? I'm kind of in a hurry, so if you could just ring me up, I'd appreciate it."

"No problem." I take the hat and scan the bar code. "That'll be $21.99."

"Thanks for coming in today," I mumble as they're on their way out the door.

The day continues on, and I do my best to improve my stats as I help the various customers who come through the door.

Finally when we have a lull in customers, I pull up our reports and run the daily stats to see how I'm doing. I'm way off the store's averages at a $25.00 *Average Sale* and 1.5 *Items per Transaction*. I need to get to an *Average Sale* of $49.00 and 2.0 *Items per Transaction*. I don't have a prayer!

Out of curiosity, I run the store sales report to see how my sales are looking for the day. To my surprise, I'm leading the store in sales for the day. I have $275 while Jimmy is at $200 and Larry is at $175. I flip back to the daily stats report. Both of them are riding above the store average in both *Average Sale* and *Items per Transaction*.

Now that's ammunition if I've ever seen any. If I'm leading the store in sales, he's got to give me a little leeway on the stats—at least he ought to.

Jimmy is finishing up his sale in the back of the store. They settle on a couple of T-shirts and a hat, putting back most of the stuff they had in their arms. The sale ends up costing $65 and being

3 items—aiding Jimmy's stats for the day but not putting him ahead of me in sales.

When he's done ringing up their sale and they've left the store, I call him over.

"Hey, Jimmy." I'm curious what he'll have to say about this. "Check this out."

I show him the stats report and smile as he starts to give me a lecture on stats.

"Just a minute," I interrupt him. "Now look at the sales report."

Jimmy pulls up the sales report and looks a little confused as he sees that I'm ahead of him by $10 in sales.

"What do you think of that?" I smile and give it a minute to sink in. "So here's the golden question. Which would you rather have: sales or stats?"

"Both." Jimmy is quick to answer.

"Okay," I continue, "so you'd like both, but if you had to pick just one, which would it be: sales or stats?"

"I've really got to deliver both," Jimmy says. "The DM said, if we can't bring up the stats, I'd be looking for a new job. I've always assumed the two deliverables would come hand in hand."

"But if you had to pick one or—put another way—if the DM had to pick one, he'd probably pick sales," I suggest. "He surely wouldn't want us to turn away people unless they were willing to spend at least $100 on 5 items, would he?"

Jimmy turns to the computer to look at the reports again.

"In our basketball game on Thursday, at the end of the game, all that really mattered was who had put more points on the board, regardless of what percentage they shot. At the end of the day in the store, all that really matters is whether or not we are getting sales, right?"

"I guess so." Jimmy is a little reticent to admit it.

"So," I say, smiling, "right now, I'm leading the store for the day—despite my stats." I don't wait for a response as I head to help some customers who are coming in the door.

The Profit Equation

The rest of the day, Jimmy and I battle it out for the most individual sales. We pick a goal that we each work toward and both of us smash them by late afternoon. I think back to the quote in English: "Keep your mind on the great and splendid thing you would like to do; and then, as the days go gliding by, you will find yourself unconsciously seizing the opportunities that are required for the fulfillment of your desire." It worked again on the sales floor, just like it had on the hardwood.

By the end of the day, Jimmy just edges me out for the top position in the store in sales, but we both smoke Larry—despite the fact that he has the best stats. I'm confident now that *Average Sale* and *Items per Transaction* aren't the cure-all measurements for the store. I'll stick with *Total Sales*, as that seems to be a nice, simple number.

I'll have to ask Coach on Monday why these stats that everyone swears by haven't panned out to be the end-all that everyone makes them out to be.

As we clean up for the night, Jimmy still looks a little worried.

"The problem is, Davis, if the DM is looking for good stats, how do we explain that we can put up good sales despite mediocre stats?"

"We'll just have to figure out a way to show him that stats don't always equal sales." I'm hoping now that Coach will be able to help us solve this problem.

"I just don't get it," Jimmy says as he wipes off the counter. "Nearly every store in this mall measures those stats. They can't all be wrong, can they?"

"I don't know. We saw it today though. Larry smoked us in the stats but didn't even sniff the sales we put up." I'm sure we're right, but I can't explain why yet.

"Well, we've got to figure it out fast. I think the DM is coming by sometime next week to see how we're progressing. If he sees that our stats are down even farther than before, he'll be beside himself. I promised we'd get 'em up and get 'em up fast. His solution to the problem was to get rid of the people who were bringing us down, like you. Now, I'm not so sure."

Jimmy finishes wiping off the counter and starts counting the till.

"We'll figure it out. I think I know just the person who can help us out. Remember Coach H., the baseball coach? I've been spending a little time talking to him this week, and he claims to have the answers to all my problems—including what to do about the store. I'll talk to him Monday, and then we can talk again when I come into work. Let's put some thought into a sales figure that would really impress the DM. Then we can show him that we can deliver great sales, no matter what the stats. He'll have to listen to our argument then."

I put on my coat and head for the gate.

"I hope you're right—for your sake and mine. See ya later, Davis. Good job today. You gave me a run for my money."

Jimmy closes the gate behind me.

As I walk out to my car, I'm feeling pretty good about life. I'm still not sure what to do from here, but I see the power of defining the goal in one clear number versus an individual, or even a collective, stat.

Chapter 12

"Good morning, Samantha. Morning, Davis. You're at it bright and early for a Monday." Coach comes up behind us and catches Samantha by surprise.

"Are you ready to take the next step?" Coach asks as he unlocks the door to his classroom. While Coach hangs up his jacket and puts a few things in his office, Samantha and I pull up a few chairs.

"So where should we start?" Coach asks. "Why don't you tell me which problem you decided to focus on, Davis, and then tell me how you defined success for that problem. Then we can move on to the next step."

"Okay, let's see. Where to start. I decided to focus on my problem at work, given the fact that my stats have been diving and my job is in jeopardy. I automatically assumed that the solution to my problem would be higher stats. I just wasn't sure which one to pick. In the last few days, I've come to see the error of my ways."

"How so?" Coach asks.

"Well, I was trying to decide between *Average Sale* and *IPT* after we talked last Thursday. Interestingly enough, as we played Hillcrest that night, I had an eye-opener that made me change my mind. Before the game, I was thinking about field goal percentage, Wally's stat of choice. I thought that I could focus on driving that stat as a little trial run to get ready to go to work and try to improve my stats there. After all, a stat is a stat, right?

"As the game got under way, I got in early foul trouble and went to the bench. When I came out of the game, I had a perfect field goal percentage. I was one for one. While I sat there, I couldn't help but think that field goal percentage couldn't be the right answer. How could I win—at least in terms of having great stats—and my team get thumped overall? It was then I realized that the solution couldn't lie in an individual or even an overall stat. It had to be much bigger than that. Real success could only be defined by a win at the end of the game.

"I picked a number of points that I thought would bring us a win, and then Slim and I went to town to reach that given point level." I smile at the memory. "The rest is history."

"That's interesting, Davis," Coach admits. "But what does that have to do with your problem at work."

"Everything, I think," I begin. "It seems like I went through a very similar process to solve my problem at work."

"How so?" Samantha asks.

"Well, I had decided that one possible solution to my problem would be a better *Average Sale*. To be exact, I was shooting for a $49 *Average Sale*, which is our store average. While I was working Saturday, I realized that, just like in our basketball game, a given individual or even team stat wasn't going to be the answer to my problem.

"As I worked with Jimmy, my boss, on Saturday he started by encouraging me to get my stats up," I explain.

I recount to Coach and Samantha how I realized midmorning that I was ahead of everyone in sales, despite the fact that my stats were terrible. I talk through the conversation we had and how we refocused our efforts on trying to put up good sales, regardless of how our stats ended up.

"At the end of the day, Jimmy and I put up great sales, while Larry only had marginal sales. Surprisingly, Larry had much better stats than Jimmy and I. I decided that a *Total Sales* figure would be the overall goal for the store. Now we just have to figure out why stats aren't, so we can explain it to our DM."

"I think that will be easy enough," Coach assures me. "Once you can show that you can consistently put up good sales numbers, the DM won't need much explanation."

The Profit Equation

"I hope you're right, Coach. The problem is I'm not sure if we can duplicate it or not. It seems like setting a single number as a goal really helped out at work and in our ball game, but I don't know if that will be enough."

Coach stands up and heads over to the board.

"Well, let's get to work. Two things I want to mention before we get going. First, I want to commend you on coming to the understanding that seldom, if ever, will an individual stat or even a team stat help you maximize your results.

"The key is that, at the end of the day, the one number you are looking for should be the one number that you can't live without. In Davis' basketball game for example, he could live without shooting percentage, as long as his score was higher than Hillcrest's score.

"It wouldn't matter if you shot 100 percent or 25 percent, if the total points you scored were less than the total points scored by the other team. At the end of the day, your total points are all that really matter."

"So what's the second thing Coach?" I'm anxious to get going on this process.

"Well, it's about your final answer to the store problem. I think you are very close with *Total Sales* but ..." He trails off as if he'd like me to finish the sentence for him.

"So it's not *Total Sales*?" I ask incredulously. "I could have sworn I was on the right track."

"It's close, Davis," Coach reassures me. "Let me ask this. If, at the end of the day, all you had were great sales would that be sufficient?"

"Jimmy seems to think so. He's mentioned in the past that his bonus is tied to *Total Sales*, and if Jimmy is getting his bonus because of my contribution, then I'm sure I'll be able to keep my job."

"Okay." Coach smiles. "I can see where you are coming from. Let's take it one step further. Let's say that you—or Jimmy in this case—weren't just the manager of the store. Let's say that you were the owner of the store. Would *Total Sales* be enough?"

"I don't see why not," I say.

"Yeah, Coach," Samantha chimes in. "It seems like, if you had great sales, everything else would fall into place."

"Well almost." Coach thinks before he goes on. "What if you were selling products for less than they cost you to buy them? Say you are selling hats that cost you $10 for $8. You could probably sell a ton of them at that price."

"Sure, you could," I admit. "But you'd be out of business in no time flat."

"So the key isn't to just have sales," Coach says. "You have to have profitable sales—sales that generate enough money over your cost to cover rent, wages, and then some."

"So the answer is *Profit*," Samantha suggests. "Instead of *Total Sales* they should be shooting for total *Profit*."

"Exactly." Coach grins. "From your point of view, the world at the store ends at sales, because you don't have to worry about the costs that go into making the store tick. At the end of the day, though, the real goal is to make a profit."

"Fair enough," I agree. "*Profit* it is. So, where do we go from here?"

"Well, now that you've identified a solution to your problem in terms of a single number and understand that no single stat will get you there, you're ready to learn the process that will help you consistently produce that number."

"Great." I'm ready to keep moving. "Let's get started."

"Alright, which one of you can remember what the word algebra means?" Coach asks.

I've got this one: "Restoration of broken parts."

"That's right. Restoration of broken parts. Now remember, Davis, when we met that first morning. I talked to you about algebra being a lot like putting together a puzzle. It was a process of taking piece A plus piece B plus piece C plus piece D to make a whole puzzle E. You have just taken the last few days and identified E. Just like when you do a puzzle, you now have in your mind what the end result should look like. Now we have to figure out what the pieces are."

The Profit Equation

"You have seen a little success already by measuring E to get you where you wanted to go. You did, however, say yourself that while you have delivered once while measuring the whole, you're not sure you can repeat the performance again—both on the court and on the sales floor. If you can identify the pieces and understand how they all fit together, you will be much more likely to solve the puzzle successfully again and again."

"So what are the pieces, Coach?" Samantha asks.

"Good question, Samantha," Coach says. "The pieces are the variables that work together to form the whole. Take for example, Davis's problem at work—he has poor stats and yet found out on Saturday that, despite his poor stats, he still had good sales. My suspicion is that the stats they are measuring—*Average Sale* and *Items per Transaction*—are pieces to the puzzle but not the whole puzzle. I'd also be willing to bet that they aren't the only pieces to the puzzle. You'll often find that, in a situation like this, when you take two figures, like *Average Sale* and *Total Sales*, which by all logical reasoning should be connected but aren't, the problem is that you're missing some of the pieces."

"So, how do you know what the pieces are or if you're missing some? And once you're confident you have all the pieces, what are you supposed to do then?" I ask.

"Well, let's talk for a minute about identifying the pieces of the puzzle," Coach says. He is still standing at the board and begins to write as he talks. "Just like if you were going to put together a jigsaw puzzle, there are a couple of things to keep in mind. I've boiled it down to three rules. Here they are:"

1. Make sure you have all the pieces
2. Make sure you don't have extra pieces (pieces from other puzzles)
3. Make sure you put the pieces together correctly

Coach sits down after he finishes writing the three rules on the board.

"Now, as you start finding the pieces to your problems, you'll find out in a hurry that people break one or all of these rules a lot of the time," Coach explains.

"Why's that Coach?" Samantha asks.

"Well, for starters, not everyone's a math teacher." Coach grins. "For the most part, people are just out there doing the best they know how. They all want to succeed, and they are using the measurements that they know to try to get to where they want to go. A lot of times, people look around and see what other people in their shoes are measuring to get to success, and they assume that the next guy knows something they don't, so they play copycat."

"Kind of like Jimmy telling me that every store in the mall measures *Average Sale* and *Items per Transaction*," I suggest. "He says they're the bread-and-butter of retail, but Saturday we proved otherwise."

"That's right." Coach smiles. "I wouldn't dismiss the measurements entirely though. Usually the measurements people use are partially right. They are just guilty of breaking rule number one; they haven't taken the time to find all of the pieces to their puzzle. They've mistakenly assumed that the individual piece is the whole puzzle in and of itself and thereby are only experiencing a fraction of the success that they could enjoy if they were to employ the process I'm teaching you.

"People also fall into the common trap of focusing on a single metric or stat that at some point in time logically seemed correlated to what they were trying to achieve. Ironically, by focusing solely on that one metric, they are actually moving farther away from the end goal instead of closer to it."

"So what about rules number two and three, Coach?" Samantha asks. "Do people break those rules too?"

"Sure." Coach nods. "All the time. Rule number one is probably the most commonly broken, but people break number two and number three as well. You'll see what I mean as you start working on identifying your pieces."

"You mean you're not going to tell us what our pieces are?" I ask.

The Profit Equation

"Don't worry. It won't be as hard as you think," Coach reassures us. "And as you go through the process of finding your own pieces, it will mean a lot more to you."

"How do we go about finding the pieces, Coach? I'm not even sure where to start." Samantha doesn't seem too confident in the next step either, and rightfully so. I'm a little confused myself.

"Well, the goal of this exercise is to build an equation that shows the relationship between each of the pieces in your puzzle. When you have all of the pieces and have them put together correctly, they will equal the end result you have spent the last few days identifying. Remember in class last week when we were trying to find out if the kid had enough money to buy lunch, to get to work and back, and then to go on a date? The end goal was the cash left after the expenses he was going to incur. The pieces were the cost of gas, the miles he had to drive, the gas mileage in his car, the cost of the date, and the amount of cash he had to start with." Coach writes the equations on the board one more time:

Amount Available for Lunch = Current Cash − Cost of Date − Cost of Gas

Then, he writes:

$$\text{Cost of Gas} = \text{Distance You Need to Drive} \times \frac{\text{Gallons of Gas}}{\text{Miles Driven}} \times \frac{\text{Cost of Gas}}{\text{Gallons of Gas}}$$

"It's really just that simple. You know the end goal. Now you just have to identify the missing variables." Coach erases the board as the first bell rings. "Really, I promise. It's a lot easier than most people think it will be."

"We'll take your word for it, Coach," Samantha says halfheartedly as she grabs her bag to head to first period.

"Thanks for the help, Coach." I stand up as well.

"You bet. Samantha, if you're game, why don't you spend some time with Davis trying to figure out the pieces to his puzzle. Like I mentioned before, once you've gone through the process once or twice, you'll be able to apply it to any problem you have.

Michael D. Batt

The pieces may be different, but the process you go through to find the pieces will be similar, no matter what problem you have. Circle back in a few days, and we'll see how things are going."

"We'll give it a try, Coach." We say together as we leave the classroom. "See you in algebra."

Chapter 13

I walk down the hall with Samantha.

"Well, where do you think we should start?" I ask.

"Maybe after algebra we can grab lunch and start sifting through the possible pieces. Coach says it's easy. Maybe we just need to dig in and try to figure it out."

"Sounds good to me." I like the sound of lunch with Samantha. Even if this algebra problem-solving thing doesn't work out, Coach is at least giving me the opportunity to spend more time with Samantha. I can't think of the last time I had lunch with a girl.

I head to English. We're reading again from our literature book. Hopefully, I can fake it through English; it's always been one of my better classes.

As I sit in English, I start to think about what the pieces of my problem might be. Coach said not to dismiss *Average Sale* or *Items per Transaction*; they might actually be valid pieces. I take out my notebook and write down these two measurements.

They both have the same figure on the bottom—transactions. I remember Coach saying something about how that makes it so you can subtract or multiply those types of numbers or something. I may have to go back and do a little review. The numbers on the top are different—one is a dollar figure and one is a number of items. I can't really remember what do in that situation. I'm sure Samantha will be able to help out there.

Coach said I was probably missing some pieces. I don't remember any other things that we've measured or even talked about at work. Maybe when I work tonight, I can ask Jimmy what he thinks.

I have more questions than answers at this point, but I guess it will all come together somehow.

When English is finally over, Samantha catches me in the hall before I head out to the auto body shop for second period.

"You won't believe what we talked about today in chemistry," Samantha says, beaming from ear to ear.

"What?"

"Equations!" Samantha smiles. "And how one particular equation—$E=mc^2$—was at the heart of the creation of the atomic bomb."

"Cool." I'm not sure how to respond. I mean atomic bombs sound cool and all, but I'm not sure what that has to do with anything, other than it is an equation and we're trying to make equations. I took chemistry last year, but I don't even remember what the m and the c stand for in that equation.

"Yeah, Albert Einstein was all about equations too. Check this out." She pulls her chemistry book out of her bag and flips open to a page with a corner folded down. "Read this."

I take the book from her and read out loud the quotation she has underlined in red.

"Pure mathematics is, in its way, the poetry of logical ideas. One seeks the most general ideas of operation, which will bring together in simple, logical, and unified form the largest possible circle of formal relationships."[2]

Now, do I admit that I have absolutely no clue what that just said, or should I try to play it cool and pretend like I got it? Luckily, Samantha is excited enough that she goes on before I have a chance to open my mouth and make a fool of myself.

"Do you see it, Andy?" Samantha can hardly contain herself. "That's what we're trying to do. We're trying to take all of these random pieces that right now seem unconnected and form logical relationships. Einstein was trying to figure out the energy

---

[2] Albert Einstein, "Emmy Noether's Obituary," New York Times, May 5, 1935.

that is pent up inside an atom. That was the single number that he was looking for. Lots of different scientists were trying to solve this problem. Finally, Einstein found the right pieces to the puzzle and the right relationship between the pieces and came up with the equation that is possibly the most universally known equation in the world. We have defined the solution for each of your problems. Now we just have to figure out the right pieces and how they go together. If we can use math to do it in a 'simple, logical, and unified form,' the end result will be an equation that will be as profoundly applicable as $E=mc^2$—well, at least, profoundly applicable for us."

Okay, clearly I am outclassed here, but I'm glad she'll be helping me. It's like the light bulb has come on for Samantha, and she gets where we have to go next. Before she can discover my ignorance, I better head to auto body.

"Sounds like you have it all under control, Samantha. I sure am glad you're helping me out with this." I push open the big double doors that lead out to the shop. "We still on for lunch?"

"Yeah. I'll see you then." Samantha practically floats off to class on her newfound confidence.

CHAPTER 14

I slide into algebra a little late and can't find a seat close enough to talk to Samantha before class. Coach is already at the board going to town solving equations. Last week, we worked on the equation for the kid who wanted to go to lunch. Luckily, today Coach is reviewing how we have to have "like terms" in order to work with multiple "pieces" in equations.

"So let's say you have two of the variables we were working with the other day."

$$\frac{1 \text{ Gallon of Gas}}{15 \text{ Miles}}$$

"And…"

$$\frac{\$2.50}{1 \text{ Gallon of Gas}}$$

"The most important thing to remember is to always include the term—or type of thing—you are working with in your equation. If I had just written this—"

$$\frac{1}{15} \quad \text{and} \quad \frac{2.50}{1}$$

"—you wouldn't have any idea how to work with these figures. Once you add the terms to the figures, you will then know what operations will work between the two figures and which ones won't. As a general rule, if the terms on the bottom and the top are the same, you can subtract or add those figures. A second rule is that, if you have the same term on the top of one figure and on the bottom of another, you can multiply those figures together."

Coach returns to the board and writes as he talks, "In the example here, we have *Gallons of Gas* on the top of one figure and the bottom of the other, so we can multiply them together, and the *Gallons of Gas* will eliminate each other, like this."

$$\frac{1 \; \cancel{\text{Gallon of Gas}}}{15 \text{ Miles}} \times \frac{\$2.50}{1 \; \cancel{\text{Gallon of Gas}}}$$

"The numbers stay and multiply with the numbers on the top or bottom respectively like this."

$$\frac{1 \times \$2.50}{15 \text{ Miles} \times 1} = \frac{\$2.50}{15 \text{ Miles}}$$

"So, now we know that it costs us $2.50 for each 15 miles we drive."

Coach erases the numbers from the board.

"There may be instances when the figures you have aren't exactly in the right order to work with. You may have to tweak the numbers you have to make them work. Say, for example, that instead of the numbers that we just had, we were given the following:"

$$\frac{15 \text{ Miles}}{1 \text{ Gallon of Gas}}$$

"And ..."

$$\frac{\$2.50}{1 \text{ Gallon of Gas}}$$

"Based on what we just discussed, we don't have the same term on the top and bottom of both figures, and we don't have a similar term on the top of one figure and the bottom of the other. There is a way to deal with something like this by using division, but for now, let's focus on addition, subtraction and multiplication. Those will be the easiest to think about."

Coach stops for a minute so we can think about what he is telling us before he continues. "The key here is that you can flip figures without changing what they mean. So, for this example let's flip the second figure, just to show you that it all works out the same."

$$\frac{\$2.50}{1 \text{ Gallon of Gas}}$$

" … is the same as …"

$$\frac{1 \text{ Gallon of Gas}}{\$2.50}$$

"We can then take the first figure and multiply it by our flipped figure like this."

$$\frac{15 \text{ Miles}}{1 \cancel{\text{Gallon of Gas}}} \times \frac{1 \cancel{\text{Gallon of Gas}}}{\$2.50}$$

"Or …"

$$\frac{15 \text{ Miles}}{\$2.50}$$

" … we can then flip our answer to get the exact same answer we had before."

$$\frac{\$2.50}{15 \text{ Miles}}$$

The Profit Equation

"Now, let's look at a quick example of an instance when you could add and subtract two figures. Say we have the following information. One car can drive 200 miles per hour while the second car can drive 60 miles per hour. How much faster can the first car drive compared to the second? Now I know this is simple, but I want to make sure you get the principle. Our figures would look like this."

$$\frac{200 \text{ Miles}}{1 \text{ Hour}}$$

$$\frac{60 \text{ Miles}}{1 \text{ Hour}}$$

"Because the terms on the top and bottom of both figures are the same, you can add or subtract the two. In this case, we want to subtract like this."

$$\frac{200 \text{ Miles}}{1 \text{ Hour}} - \frac{60 \text{ Miles}}{1 \text{ Hour}} = \frac{140 \text{ Miles}}{1 \text{ Hour}}$$

Coach turns back to the class.

"If you can remember these few basic principles, it will help you solve a lot of your equations."

As Coach erases the board, he tells us to spend the rest of class working on our assignments.

I open up my binder and look back through the notes I made in English about the metrics at work.

$$\text{Average Sale} = \frac{\text{Total Sales}}{\text{Total Transactions}}$$

$$\text{Items per Transaction} = \frac{\text{Total Items}}{\text{Total Transactions}}$$

Based on what Coach said, I could flip one of these figures and then multiply the two together. I start writing.

$$\frac{\text{Total Sales}}{\cancel{\text{Total Transactions}}} \times \frac{\cancel{\text{Total Transactions}}}{\text{Total Items}} = \frac{\text{Total Sales}}{\text{Total Items}}$$

I guess I could call this "*Average Price of an Item Sold.*" I'm not sure that gets me any closer to my complete equation. Maybe I should start by figuring out all of the potential puzzle pieces so I avoid breaking the rule about leaving out pieces.

I start to jot down a few ideas, but I'm interrupted by the bell. It seems like just last week that algebra lasted an eternity. Now I wish I had a little more time to work on my equations.

Samantha comes over as I finish putting my books away.

"So, Andy, where should we go for lunch?"

"Well, if we want to talk, Molly's is probably too loud."

Molly's is really the only place to eat that's close enough to the school to get there and back in time for fifth period.

"We have some pizza in my fridge from dinner last night," Samantha offers. "What if we just run over to my house and heat it up in the microwave?"

Not exactly a romantic first date, but I guess if we want to start talking through the puzzle pieces to my problem, we need a quiet place to talk.

"Sounds good. I can drive, if you don't mind being seen in my beater."

"Oh, I don't care about that," Samantha assures me.

"Great. Well, let's get going." I open the double doors that lead to the parking lot and let Samantha go through.

As we pull up to the red brick house with Wilmington stenciled on the mailbox, Mr. Wilmington is standing in the driveway, talking to a man on a motorcycle. I hurry around the car to open the passenger door for Samantha. They stop talking as I let Samantha out of the car, and we walk toward the house.

"Hi, Dad. You remember Andy Davis, right?"

"Davis ... sure. Andy, how are you?" Mr. Wilmington is a preacher at a local church. My parents actually used to take us to Mr. Wilmington's church a few years back. Then life got busy, and we went less and less—and finally not at all.

"Doing well, Mr. Wilmington. Thanks for asking."

"We just stopped by for lunch, Dad," Samantha interrupts. "We probably need to hurry and eat so we can get back for fifth period."

"Sounds good," Mr. Wilmington says. "Before you go inside, let me introduce you to Ernie. He's the newest convert in our church."

"Nice to meet you, Ernie," Samantha and I both say as we shake hands with the man.

"Nice to meet you two as well," Ernie says. He looks a little rough around the edges, but he seems nice enough. We hurry inside, and Samantha takes the leftover pizza out of the fridge and puts it in the microwave.

I pull out my notebook and leaf through the pages while I wait for her to come back.

"So what does a person do to be a convert in your dad's church?" I ask as Samantha brings the pizza to the table.

"I'm not really sure," Samantha says. "Dad's told me a little bit about this Ernie guy. Sounds like he's led quite the life. He lived in a big city for the last several years and ran with a pretty rough crowd. He decided it was time to clean up his life, so he went looking for a job in a smaller town where he could start fresh. Dad ran into him a few months ago over at Molly's and suggested Ernie ought to come by the church on Sundays and see what he thought. Ernie showed up the next Sunday and has been coming ever since. Dad says it's pretty amazing to see the change that has come over him in such a short amount of time."

"Sounds interesting," I admit. We take a few minutes to eat as we continue to talk about Ernie.

"Well, we better start talking about your job, before we need to get back," Samantha says, shifting gears. "Where should we start?"

"I started thinking about it earlier during class. Right now, we measure *Average Sale* and *Items per Transaction*. In order to measure these, we have to measure a few other things to make the calculations work—like *Total Sales*, *Total Items Sold*, and *Total Transactions*. I'm guessing there are some other things we could measure as well."

"Like what?"

"I don't know. Maybe *Hours Worked*, *Number of Employees*, ... *Number of Customers* who come in the store. I guess we could measure the *Amount of Inventory* that we have in our store; you have to have stuff to sell stuff."

"Those sound like reasonable things." Samantha watches as I jot down the things I just suggested. "As we talked about Einstein in chemistry today, I wondered how he finally figured out the pieces to his puzzle. I wonder if he went through a similar process."

We sit in silence for a few minutes as we look back over the list of things on my paper. Somehow, we have to take all of these pieces and "bring [them] together in simple, logical, and unified form" just like Einstein did. We need to find the relationships between the pieces that will make them equal *Profit* at the end of the day. It sounds like quite a daunting task.

Samantha stands up and takes our plates to the sink.

"We better get back to school if we want to make it to fifth period."

I'd rather stay here and keep talking, but I guess if I'm hanging out with the future valedictorian, I'll have to live with the fact that I won't be skipping many classes.

Ernie fires up his motorcycle as Samantha and I come out the front door. I can definitely see him running with a rough crowd in his former life. He has long hair pulled back in a ponytail, and he still sports a nice leather jacket and leather pants.

We walk into the school just as the warning bell rings. I work tonight, and then Samantha is coming over when I get off so we can continue to work on identifying the pieces to my puzzle.

Chapter 15

Jimmy is waiting for me when I get to work.

"Davis. Man, am I glad you're here! The last two days have been rough. I've thought a lot about what we discovered on Saturday and have been trying to duplicate it, but without any luck."

"How so?" I grin. "You must need me around to make it happen."

"Who knows? Maybe you are the missing link." Jimmy looks concerned. "Yesterday and today, I've set goals for our sales and tried to focus more on that than on my stats. The result? Bad sales and bad stats. I'm pretty confident that, if we don't have good sales, we'll have a hard time arguing with the DM that good stats aren't really that important."

"Yeah, I hear what you're saying. I'm hopeful that tonight I can nail down some of the other things we should measure and then try to figure out how they might actually help us reach our end goal of *Profit*. I also need to catch you up to speed on why we should focus on *Profit* and not just *Total Sales*."

It's an easy sell. Jimmy has no problem agreeing that we need to focus on overall profitability. He says, as the manager of the store, he is also responsible for making sure that we aren't discounting too much, using too many labor hours, or wasting supplies. For the most part, he just does that on the back end and focuses with the staff on sales.

"So, any suggestions on how we can consistently produce good profit with or without good stats?" Jimmy asks as we finish talking about profit. "I think the DM is planning to come again later this week. I'd like to have an answer of some sort and hopefully some numbers to back it up. Saturday was solid, but yesterday and today, we were way off what I was hoping to put up."

"Well, I met with Coach H. this morning, and I've been working on some of the things he said we need to focus on next." I pull the notebook out of my bag; I brought it so I could show Jimmy my notes. Luckily—or maybe in this case unluckily—the mall isn't too busy on Monday nights, and we should have a little time to talk through some of the things we ought to measure.

I set the notebook on the counter and open it to the page where I'd listed the things to measure.

"So Coach said the next step, now that we've identified the single number we're working toward, is to identify all of the things that we might measure that would help us get to our goal. The way he puts it, we need to build an equation that explains how to accomplish our goal."

"So what kind of an equation?"

"I'm not quite sure yet. All I know now is that we need to identify the different pieces. Here are the ones I wrote down today." I slide him the notebook and let him read through my list.

> Sales
> Transactions
> Average Sale
> Items Sold
> Customers
> Employees
> Hours Worked
> Inventory on Hand

We add *Cost of Goods Sold* to get us closer to *Profit*.

"Can you think of other items we might measure?" I ask as he finishes reading the list.

The Profit Equation

"Well, I know from time to time they've measured *Total Labor Expense*—usually as a function of sales—so *Labor Expense* divided by *Sales*. They've also measured *Sales per Hours Worked* and *Sales per Hour the Store is Open*. These measurements usually last for a few months, and then they die off, and nobody ever asks about them again."

I add these to my list.

Labor Expense
Sales per Hours Worked
Sales per Hours the Store is Open

As I finish writing, I have a question for Jimmy.

"Why do you think these measurements come and go? It seems like programs in general seem to be like that. They're born, live a short life, and then fall by the wayside."

"I guess somebody gets a notion that one of these new stats will drive awareness of an item that has gotten out of control. We swing the pendulum so far and make such a big deal of it that the problem gets fixed while everything else gets out of whack. The pendulum then swings back the other way, and the focus shifts to the next new problem until it is fixed. We seem to be in this constant mode of fire fighting—trying to solve the problems that we created while we were focused so heavily on the last fire!"

I can tell that Jimmy has lived through a few pendulum swings, and probably that fact alone makes each new swing less effective, since all involved are confident that the emphasis will probably be short-lived.

"Can you think of anything else we might measure?" I ask. "I think if we can identify all of the potential things, then it will be easier to put together this equation that Coach wants us to build."

"Nothing that I can think of. Let me think about it though, and maybe I'll remember something else as the night goes on."

I only work for about four hours tonight, and I'm not sure how late Jimmy is planning on working. He's been working open to close a lot lately, and I can tell that it's starting to wear on him.

I put the notebook under the counter and head over to the hat wall. Most Monday nights, my job is to go through and tidy up the wall and make sure that all of the hats are organized by team and style, and then arrange them from biggest to smallest.

Jimmy heads over to refold some T-shirts while I dig into the hat wall. I've got a knack for mixing up the wall so it looks fresh and draws customers' eyes as they walk through the store. Some guys can't stand this job, but I actually like it and often find myself lost in my work, oblivious to anything else that's going on around.

Tonight is no different, and I'm on cruise control somewhere between the Louisville and Connecticut section when I'm startled by a tap on the shoulder.

"Excuse me, son."

I hate it when old guys call me son.

"Could you tell me if you have any Steelers sweatshirts?"

When I set down the stack of hats I was working on, I'm surprised to find that the customer who tapped my shoulder is none other than Ernie, Mr. Wilmington's new convert.

"Sure. Right over here. Let me show you what we have." I lead him through the maze of floor fixtures to the NFL section. "It's Ernie, right?"

He looks at me—a little surprised that I know his name. He probably doesn't recognize me in my work jersey with a baseball hat. I take off my hat and stick out my hand.

"I met you today over at the Wilmington's. Andy Davis—but most people call me Davis."

"That's right. Sorry I didn't recognize you."

"No problem."

I pull out a few different styles of Steelers sweatshirts that we currently carry.

"So what brings you into the store today?" I ask. "Looking for a gift?"

"Yeah." Ernie holds up a solid black, hooded sweatshirt with the Steelers emblem embroidered on the front. "I've got a friend from back in my hometown who's going through a rough time, and I wanted to find something to cheer him up."

"That's a great sweatshirt. I'd imagine that would do the trick. If you're a Steelers fan, that is." I have to throw in a snide remark now and then to Steelers fans to get them worked up.

"Yeah, I'm not a huge Steelers fan myself, but I suppose if a friend needs a pick-me-up, it wouldn't do him much good if I sent him my team's sweatshirt." Ernie winks at me and motions to the Raider's hat I'm wearing.

"I guess that's true."

Ernie spends a few minutes looking at the sweatshirts while I migrate back to the hat wall. I'm curious to learn more about what made Ernie decide to change his life around. I can't imagine a guy going from being a hard-core biker to a church-goer. Something must have happened that made him want to turn things around. I'm just not sure if that's a conversation that you can strike up with someone you've never talked to.

I guess we're both Raiders fans, though, so why not. I slowly make my way back over to Ernie, who looks like he's settled on a sweatshirt for his friend.

"So if it's not too forward, I was wondering if I could ask you a question."

"Sure. No problem. What can I do for you?"

"Well, Samantha, Mr. Wilmington's daughter, was telling me today that you moved from the big city recently to kind of start over. I imagine that's quite a transition. I was hoping you could tell me what made you decide to change."

"I don't know that there's time enough in the day—or even the week—to give that question a fair answer. It's an awful long story."

"So how 'bout the *Reader's Digest* version?"

"Well, I reckon it's never just one thing. The long and the short of it is, I was headed on a one-way track to jail and finally came to my senses that I didn't want to spend the rest of my days behind bars." Ernie pauses as he thinks about what to say. "A good buddy of mine recently got caught dealing, and they locked him away. I guess that was the beginning. I decided to get out. I needed a new start and knew I'd never get it in the big city. Things seem to work that way; you get in a rut, and it's awful hard to get out. Whenever you try, the others in the rut pull you back in."

"So how did you get out?"

"Well, one night I just bailed. I packed a few things and jumped on the train. Didn't tell a soul I was leaving or where I was going. After a few hours on the train, I pulled into the station here and decided this looked like as good a place as any to start over."

"You just up and left, huh?"

"Yep. I figured it was the only way to do it."

I wonder what you do when you land in a brand new town coming from a life like that.

Ernie finally continued, "The next morning, I went out and got a job as a hired hand on a farm on the outskirts of town. They were the only folks who would give me a shot; I guess they needed help real bad. Not too many places look too favorable on a rough-lookin' guy like me."

"So what happened next?"

"Well, I worked on the farm for a few weeks and got myself cleaned up a little. I realized my life wasn't all that I thought it would end up as. I decided I needed something else. I started visiting a few different churches in town. Nothing seemed quite right—or like I really fit in."

"What made you start coming to Mr. Wilmington's church, then?"

"Well, I guess it was Mr. Wilmington himself. He accepted me right from the start—no judgment on where I'd come from or what I'd done. His sermons were down to earth and just what I needed as I was in this process of turning my life around." Ernie clearly had a great amount of respect for Mr. Wilmington.

"So, Mr. Wilmington said that you were the newest convert in his church. I've been wondering … what exactly is a convert? How does somebody become converted?"

"I'm not exactly sure. I've heard the term several times since I started coming to church, but I guess I've never viewed myself as a convert. I reckon it just means that I used to be one type of person, and now I'm in this process of converting myself into a new type of person, a different type of person. The church is helping me in the conversion process."

Ernie takes his sweatshirt and heads to the counter. When we get to the counter, I take the sweatshirt from him and ring it up.

"I don't know if I really answered your question or not, son." Ernie takes his bag as I hand it over the counter. "It's really been quite the ride. I'm a completely different person from the guy I was six months ago. I think I'm adjusting to the changes, and it sure is a better alternative than being behind bars."

"Thank you."

I'm very impressed with Ernie and his sincerity and kindness. "You've been more than helpful, and I appreciate you humoring my questions."

"Anytime." Ernie sticks out his hand to shake mine. "Maybe we'll see you around the church sometime."

"Yeah. Maybe so." I imagine the more I hang out with Samantha the more likely I'll be to go to church one of these days.

After Ernie leaves the store, Jimmy stops folding T-shirts to come and talk to me.

"Hey, I couldn't help but overhear as you talked to that guy. It helped me remember one other thing that some of the retailers in the mall measure from time to time: *Conversion Rate*."

"Conversion rate? What's that?"

"It's the rate at which you can get shoppers to become buyers. I think it's calculated by dividing the total number of transactions that you have in a day by the total number of shoppers who come in your store that day."

"So why don't we measure conversion rate now?" I ask.

"Well, we used to have a customer counter, but it broke. I guess we never got around to fixing it, and that fad died like the rest of them."

"Jimmy, I think that's it. I think that's our missing piece."

"How do you figure?" Jimmy looks a little confused.

Michael D. Batt

"Can I take off early tonight?" I plead. "I need a little time to work through this on paper, and then I'll come back on Wednesday and tell you what I figure out. I think we can explain to the DM how we can make this store crank out the sales again."

Jimmy looks around and realizes that there aren't many customers around, so he agrees.

"As long as you can fix our problem, get going. I'll expect a lot on Wednesday, so you better come through."

"Don't worry. I will." I grab my bag and coat and head for the entrance. "See you Wednesday."

CHAPTER 16

I make a beeline for the parking lot and fire up my old beast. Samantha was going to come over at nine o'clock when I should have gotten off work, but I'm almost an hour early. Maybe I'll just swing by her house and see if she can come now.

As I drive, I start thinking through this conversion rate idea. I remember that we talked about conversion last year in chemistry; I hope Samantha can help out with the details. In essence, I remember that it was the process of converting a measurement of one type into a measurement of another type, like inches to feet or grams to pounds.

It's just like with Ernie, changing a person of one type into a person of another type. And also just like the conversion rate in the store, changing one type of person—a shopper—into another type of person—a buyer.

I guess it's really just the same as what we were working on today in algebra when we were multiplying the different things together to end up with what we wanted.

Converting from one type of thing to another is the way that we can start linking the different pieces that Samantha and I listed out earlier today. We know what we want—that was Coach H.'s first assignment. Now we've started working on what we have. We can use this concept of conversion to change what we have into what we want. I can hardly wait to talk to Samantha.

I run to her front door and ring the doorbell. Her mom comes to the door.

"Hello, Mrs. Wilmington. Is Samantha home?" I've only met her mom a time or two, but she's as nice as Mr. Wilmington.

"Yes, just a moment. Won't you come in?" Mrs. Wilmington opens the door and shows me into the living room. I feel a little out of place in their fancy living room with their grand piano and me in my work uniform. The Wilmington's are definitely classy people.

I sit down on the couch while Mrs. Wilmington goes to get Samantha. I still can't believe that I'm actually sitting in the living room of Samantha Wilmington.

After a few minutes, Samantha comes down stairs. I can hardly wait to tell her the things I've learned.

"Hi, Andy. What are you doing off work so early? You didn't get fired did you?" Samantha looks worried.

"No, not at all." I smile at her. "I ran into Ernie, your dad's friend, at work tonight, and I think he helped me know what we need to do next."

"Who would have guessed that Ernie was a math guy? I mean, he's nice and all; I just wouldn't pick him out as an algebra junkie."

"Well, it wasn't exactly like that," I say. "We started talking about what made him change his life around. What made him decide to convert to your dad's church."

"So what does that have to do with our equations?"

"Well, everything, I think. I'm guessing that it's the missing piece to the puzzle. Why don't we go grab something to eat, and I can explain on the way?"

"Sure." Samantha heads back down the hallway. "Let me tell my parents I'm going out, and I'll be right back."

"Sounds good." I'm excited to see what she thinks of my latest idea.

When she comes back, we head out to the car and decide to get takeout from a small Chinese place.

As we leave her driveway, I start the explanation, "So, you ready to hear what I think?"

"Yeah, let's hear it."

"So what type of person did Ernie used to be?"

"Pretty hard-core, I guess," Samantha says.

"That's right. And what kind of a person is he now?" I ask.

"Well, from what I can tell he's a pretty nice guy."

"That's right. So what made him change? I mean how does a guy like Ernie go from being pretty hard-core to being a pretty nice guy?"

"I imagine it was a long process," Samantha says. "Not something that happened over night."

"Exactly; it was a process." I'm grinning from ear to ear. "Remember, I asked you earlier how someone became a convert in your dad's church? I didn't think of this until later, but to convert means to change from one thing to another. You probably have done conversions in chemistry."

"Yeah, we just finished talking about that."

"Good, because I think I'm going to need your help. At work, we talk about conversion as well. At one point, the store was measuring conversion rate—the rate at which we convert shoppers into buyers."

"So I'm still not exactly sure how this is the piece that will bring everything together. What are you trying to tell me?"

"Sorry, I tend to ramble when I'm excited. Let me back up a little and try to explain." I take a deep breath and start over. "The very first time Coach H. met with me, he told me that the definition of algebra was restoration of broken parts. He said it was like putting a puzzle back together."

"Yeah, I remember that," Samantha says.

"Coach said that the first step was to figure out what the finished puzzle looked like. That wasn't too hard, and I think we can both agree that to have an end goal in mind is valuable all by itself. The problem was that we didn't have a good way to make sure that we could replicate the results each time."

"Yeah," Samantha says. "The end goal was powerful but not instructive in and of itself."

"That's right," I continue, "so then Coach talked to us about identifying pieces. He taught us that there were three things to watch out for."

"Too many pieces, not enough pieces, or pieces in the wrong order," Samantha chimes in.

"We listed out several of the different pieces today at lunch," I say. "What I wasn't sure about was how I would know if I was breaking one of Coach's three rules. As I talked to Ernie tonight, for some reason, it clicked."

"Okay," Samantha says, nodding, "but what does conversion have to do with it?"

"Well, when you put together a puzzle—say a simple six-piece puzzle—, how long does it take you to figure out if you have extra pieces or missing pieces or if you have put them together correctly?" I ask.

"A few seconds I guess."

"That's right." I smile. "But if you never try to put the pieces together, would you know if you have any problems with your pieces?"

"I guess not," Samantha says.

"So the way we figure out the puzzle is we start putting it together. As we go along, we will quickly be able to identify what pieces we need and which ones we don't." I still haven't answered her question about conversion, yet so I give that a stab. "So your question was 'What does conversion have to do with it?'

"Conversion is the process that we will use to put the pieces together to get the end result. It's really more than just putting the pieces together though—it's changing the individual pieces into the finished puzzle. Just like if you had a bunch of puzzle pieces and put them all together. You wouldn't say, 'Those are a bunch of cool pieces'; you'd say, 'That's a beautiful picture of a car or a boat.' In chemistry, when you convert two chemicals into a third chemical, you don't necessarily have the original chemicals anymore. They change and become part of something new."

"I think I'm starting to get what you're saying. Let's try it out to make sure I'm with you."

The Profit Equation

We've been sitting outside the Chinese place for a few minutes as we've continued to talk. I'm starving and confident that I can work better on a full stomach.

"Let's grab dinner and head over to my house, and I'll show you what I mean."

I open her door for her, and we run in to get our food.

I'm a huge fan of the sweet and sour pork, and Samantha orders kung pao chicken. The service is great, and in no time, we're headed to my house. We hurry inside and sit at the kitchen table. I pull out some paper to make our first equation while we eat.

"First off, on the right-hand side of the equation, let's write down what we are trying to achieve—our single number end goal. In this case, let's start with words, and we'll put in numbers later."

"Okay." Samantha takes over and grabs the pencil as I dish up the food. "In this case our end goal is *Profit*. So I guess the equation would look like this."

= Profit

"Great." I give Samantha her food in exchange for the pencil. "Now let's review the pieces that we identified earlier that we could possibly measure. I added a few tonight with Jimmy.

Sales
Transactions
Average Sale
Items Sold
Customers
Employees
Hours Worked
Inventory on Hand
Labor Expense
Sales per Hours Worked
Sales per Hours Store is Open
Conversion Rate
Cost of Goods Sold

Michael D. Batt

"It's probably fair to say that our first piece has to be customers who come through our doors. So let's start building the left-hand side."

$$\text{Customers} = \text{Profit}$$

"Now if I remember right, in chemistry, if we want to convert one foot into inches, we need to multiply the one-foot measurement by the appropriate ratio: 12 inches over 1 foot. If we apply the same principle to this situation, we need to multiply the *Customers* who come through our door by a ratio, or series of ratios, that will leave us with *Profit* on the right-hand side. Obviously, at this point, we don't have a *Profit per Customer* stat, so what do you think we need to convert *Customers* into so that we eventually get to *Profit*?" I ask.

"Well, I think you said yourself that they used to measure *Conversion Rate* in the store. We could multiply *Customers* by *Transactions per Customer*."

"That sounds reasonable," I agree. I add to my equation:

$$\text{Customers} \times \frac{\text{Transactions}}{\text{Customers}} = \text{Profit}$$

"So if we cross off the like terms, we are left with something like this."

$$\cancel{\text{Customers}} \times \frac{\text{Transactions}}{\cancel{\text{Customers}}} = \text{Profit}$$

"Now we have to figure out how to convert *Transactions* into *Profit*."

Samantha slides my notebook over and looks through my list of things to measure.

"So what do you think we do next?" she asks.

The Profit Equation

"Well," I say, "We could multiply by *Items per Transaction*—the bread-and-butter of retail."

$$\text{Customers} \times \frac{\text{Transactions}}{\text{Customers}} \times \frac{\text{Items}}{\text{Transactions}} = \text{Profit}$$

"So now we have *Items* equals *Profit*. I think we're getting closer. What do you think comes next?"

Samantha looks through my list again. "We could probably add *Sales* in at this point. We could multiply by *Sales per Items Sold*—kind of like an average price of items sold."

"Okay." I add to the equation.

$$\text{Customers} \times \frac{\text{Transactions}}{\text{Customers}} \times \frac{\text{Items}}{\text{Transactions}} \times \frac{\text{Sales}}{\text{Items}} = \text{Profit}$$

"So now we have *Sales* equals *Profit*, which is obviously getting closer than when we started with *Customers* equals *Profit*," I observe. "Now we just need to convert *Sales* into *Profit*. If we multiply *Sales* by *Profit* over *Sales*, we will be left with *Profit*. This last factor will represent how much profit we make on each dollar of sales we generate."

$$\text{Customers} \times \frac{\text{Transactions}}{\text{Customers}} \times \frac{\text{Items}}{\text{Transactions}} \times \frac{\text{Sales}}{\text{Items}} \times \frac{\text{Profit}}{\text{Sales}} = \text{Profit}$$

We lean back and admire our equation. After a few minutes, I break the silence, *"The Profit Equation*—a clear, concise equation that defines how we get to our end *Profit*. Not bad. Not bad at all."

"So, Andy," Samantha interrupts my excitement at finishing the equation, "the problem is we still have ten other variables that we aren't even considering here. What about the rest?"

I don't know. It does seem a little too easy, but I'm not sure what's wrong with it. We start with *Customers*, and we end with *Profit*—that is what we were trying to do.

"I'm not sure," I admit. "Everything looks right, but I'm with you. There seems to be too much left over."

Just then my dad comes in.

"Hi, Samantha," he says. "How are you this evening?"

"I'm doing well, Mr. Davis, thank you."

"I hate to break things up, but it's almost ten o'clock, and tonight's a school night."

It's a stupid rule, I think. Who has a ten o'clock curfew besides me? But a rule's a rule in my house, and there's no point in arguing. I clean up the remains of dinner and throw away the trash.

"I'll run Samantha home and be home in a bit," I tell dad as we head for the door.

As we drive toward Samantha's, we don't say much. I'm a little stumped. I hope that we can catch Coach H. in the morning and that he can help us figure out what we need to do next with my equation. I feel pretty good about where we ended.

Finally, she breaks the silence. "So, do you think Coach will be in early tomorrow? I'd like to talk to him sooner than later."

"Yeah, me too," I agree. "Let's try to catch him before school."

As we pull up to her house, I decide it's now or never.

"Hey, would you like to go with me to a movie or something on Saturday night?" I probably sound like an idiot—I don't even know if she likes movies.

"Sure," she says. "That sounds like fun."

"Great!"

Wow! She actually said yes. Who'd believe that Samantha Wilmington would agree to go on a date with Andy Davis?

I get out of the car and let her out. I'm not sure if I should walk her to the door or not, so I just stand there like a kid who just won the lottery—too shocked to say or do anything—as Samantha walks to her house and goes inside.

I jump in the car and head home. Luckily, no cops are on the road tonight. Who can blame a kid for speeding though, when he just got a date with Samantha Wilmington?

CHAPTER 17

"Come on in." Coach motions to us as we open the door. "I thought you two might come by this morning."

"Oh yeah? What made you think that?" I ask.

"Well, once you start down the road of solving your problems using algebra, you kind of catch a bug." Coach smiles. "I thought I saw it in your eyes yesterday in class, so I just had a hunch you'd try to catch me before school today."

"You're right," Samantha says. "We met yesterday during lunch and then again last night. We think you'll be pretty proud of what we came up with. Andy calls it *The Profit Equation*."

"Well, let's see it," Coach says as he sits down in a desk near the front.

I pull out the papers we were working on last night, and we walk him through the equation we made. He doesn't say much, but I get the feeling he's pretty impressed with what we've done.

As Coach sits and looks at our equations, Samantha asks, "So, what do you think? Are we on the right track?"

"What do you think?" Coach asks in return.

"It seems right to me," I say. We spend a few minutes explaining the process that we went through to get the equation we did, explaining how we listed all of the variables and then describing my encounter with Ernie and how it got us thinking about the conversion process.

"I think this is perfect, you guys." Coach beams. "It really wasn't that hard after all, was it?"

"No, not really," Samantha says. "There are still a few things that we're not quite sure about."

"Oh yeah? What's bothering you?"

"Well," I say, "when we started working on the equation for my store, we ended up with a bunch of pieces that we didn't use. It just seemed a little bit weird. We know you said that one of the rules of building an equation was that we had to make sure we didn't use variables that didn't fit. We just didn't think there would be so many."

"That's a fair concern." Coach grins. "First, let me ask you: does your equation get you where you want to go?"

"Yes. It takes us from *Customers* to *Profit*." Samantha answers him this time.

"So, why are you worried that you are leaving pieces out of the equation?" Coach asks.

"Well," I venture, "it just seems like there are some pieces—like *Average Sale* or *Sales per Hour*—that would be logical parts of the equation but currently don't seem to fit in very well."

"Okay," Coach says after thinking for a minute. "I hear what you're saying. My problem is that one of the most common blunders that people run into—whether it's in business or sports or even right here in class—is that they force pieces. They feel so emotionally attached to a stat or even just think that the piece should logically be a part of the equation that they tend to go ahead and measure it, even if they can't make it fit in the equation."

"So, are you saying that these measurements aren't part of the equation?" Samantha asks.

"No, not at all," Coach says. "What I am saying is that if you can't find a way to make it fit in your equation, then you shouldn't measure it just because. One of my favorite sayings goes something like this: 'If you measure everything, you measure nothing.' I've been involved with too many businesses and organizations that measure things just because they can. Remember, you should *never* measure something just because you can; it always has to fit within your equation."

Michael D. Batt

I think I follow what coach is saying, but I'm not sure what more we could do with our equation. It seems to be everything he is explaining and doesn't really need any more pieces.

Coach continues, "You'll find that you can often fit in some of the extra pieces to help you better understand your equation. Let me try to give you an example. Pretend that we have an equation to build a car. It might look something like this."

$$Body + Engine + Interior + Wheels = Car$$

"This equation by itself is an accurate equation. If I were the mechanic, though, this would not be sufficient to help me build the car. I might need to break the equation down a little further like this."

$$Frame + Doors + Windows = Body$$

$$Block + Pistons + Fuel\ Injection\ System = Engine$$

$$Seats + Dash + Mats = Interior$$

$$Rims + Tires + Hubcaps = Wheels$$

"We could then combine each of the components to make a more detailed equation like this."

$$(Frame + Doors + Windows) + (Block + Pistons + Fuel\ Injection\ Sytem) + \ldots = Car$$

"Depending on the level we are working at, different amounts of detail will be more applicable. Just remember that, at every level, we can only include pieces that fit into the equation at that level. We also have to ensure on an ongoing basis that we don't add pieces that don't fit, like adding wings to our car equation."

I think I get it.

The Profit Equation

"So Coach, are you saying that some of the pieces that we weren't able to fit in our equation might actually be components of the pieces that we have?"

"Exactly," Coach says. "The other thing that you'll find is that some of the items you have on your list might already be broken down in your equation."

"Yeah," I say. "I noticed that last night. When we built our equation, we didn't include *Average Sale*, but earlier in the day, I realized that *Average Sale* was really just a combination of *Items per Transaction* and *Average Price of an Item Sold*—or *Sales per Item*. If our equation for *Average Sale* looks like this …"

$$\frac{\text{Items}}{\text{Transactions}} \times \frac{\text{Sales}}{\text{Items}} = \frac{\text{Sales}}{\text{Transactions}}$$

" … and our equation for the store right now looks like this…"

$$\text{Customers} \times \frac{\text{Transactions}}{\text{Customers}} \times \frac{\text{Items}}{\text{Transactions}} \times \frac{\text{Sales}}{\text{Items}} \times \frac{\text{Profit}}{\text{Sales}} = \text{Profit}$$

" … we could change our store equation like this:"

$$\text{Customers} \times \frac{\text{Transactions}}{\text{Customers}} \times \frac{\text{Sales}}{\text{Transactions}} \times \frac{\text{Profit}}{\text{Sales}} = \text{Profit}$$

"Exactly," Coach says. "And if you started your equation with *Average Sale* instead of the two components, you might decide to break out the equation and monitor how many items you had per transaction and how much, on average, those items cost.

"So now the question is," Coach says, sitting back and putting his hands behind his head, "which equation is more beneficial? Do we get added benefit by making our equation longer or shorter? There will be times when making the equation more complex really does make sense. Other times, it just makes it more complex."

"How can you know what the right balance is, Coach?" I ask.

"Well, there isn't just one right answer," Coach says. "A lot of times, you will need to develop your equation and then give it a few weeks or months to see if you are getting the change in results that you want. The correct equation is the equation that drives results. Period."

"Are there any other tweaks that we could make to the equation—either to make it more simple or more complex?" Samantha asks.

"Sure. You'll find that the equation can become very complex," Coach says. "For example, you may decide that number of *Customers* isn't enough. You could break that part of the equation into something much more complex like this."

Coach walks to the board and writes an equation.

$$\text{People in Town} \times \frac{\text{People Visiting Mall}}{\text{People in Town}} \times \frac{\text{Customers}}{\text{People Visting Mall}} = \text{Customers}$$

"You could then substitute this into the equation on your paper for the *Customers* variable," Coach concludes. "A marketing group might find this addition extremely helpful as it tries to assess how many people are in the town, how many of those come to the mall, and then of those, how many actually come to the store."

"But as a regular store employee, this addition doesn't really do anything for me," I add.

"That's right," Coach agrees. "For you, this addition only complicates the equation and takes your focus off of what's important. For you, the equation is more motivating and clear without the customer piece broken out."

"So, can there be more than one equation for different people?" Samantha asks.

"Kind of," Coach says. "The key is that the equation for any one group always has to equal the same ending result. So, in this case, the marketing department may have one version of the equation, the purchasing department may have a different version of the equation, and the sales associates may have yet another version of the equation. In the end, every equation is really the exact same equation, only with differing levels of detail. And every equation, in this case, ultimately equals *Profit*." Coach pauses for a minute to let that soak in.

"One of the common problems that organizations encounter is that they assume each group should only see or be measured on its piece of the puzzle. Marketing, for example, would only be evaluated on number of *Customers*, purchasing would only be evaluated on *Average Price of an Item*, and the sales department would only be evaluated on *Items per Transaction* or *Average Sale*. The assumption is that, if each person can drive his or her piece of the puzzle, then the overall puzzle will ultimately come together."

"That seems logical, Coach," I say. "Actually that sounds exactly like how we are set up at the store. Each group is responsible for its specific area."

"The problem is that what you end up getting is local optimization—maximization of the pieces, not of the whole."

"Shouldn't maximization of the pieces also maximize the whole?" Samantha asks.

"Not at all, actually." Coach smiles. "Take Davis's store for example. Let's assume that we have the three departments we just talked about—marketing, purchasing, and sales—and that they are each measured on their respective measurement—*Customers*, *Average Price of an Item*, and *Items per Transaction* or *Average Sale*."

"You're not too far from the truth," I say, thinking about how we are set up down at the store.

"With each group now focused on maximizing its piece of the puzzle, let's talk through what might—and probably will—happen. Marketing starts to come up with crazy promotions to drive traffic to the store. They propose a promotion in which they are going to give away a cruise if a customer comes into the store and fills out a form. Hoards of people show up to fill out this form, and marketing is lauded as heroes for driving traffic to the store.

"In the meantime, purchasing is trying to increase the average price of items sold. The logical way to do this is to upgrade your inventory. Purchasing used to focus on the less expensive replica jerseys but decides that if they carry more authentic jerseys, it will force people to upgrade. They decide to shift their purchasing behavior accordingly across the various product lines. Overall the average price of an item sold increases by over $5—another huge victory.

"The sales associates—who are focused solely on *Items per Transaction* and *Average Sale*—notice that they will be rewarded if they become more selective about who they sell to. They begin to profile shoppers into different categories and only help certain customers. They focus on only helping those individuals who are willing to buy multiple items or more expensive items. Employees with poor stats, like Davis here, end up getting the oust, because they are bringing down the average. Overall, the store's *Items per Transaction* and *Average Sale* increase 10 percent, and management recognizes the store employees for their significant increase.

"However, when all is said and done, overall sales have decreased significantly. What has actually happened is that, while the majority of the pieces were getting maximized, the whole has suffered. Customers came in the store in droves to fill out the new form but ended up not purchasing for a few reasons. First, they weren't the type of customer that liked sports stuff in the first place; they just wanted to go on a cruise. Second, all of the items were too expensive, because purchasing was trying to drive *Average Price of an Item Sold*. Third, they couldn't find help to save their lives, because the associates were hiding behind the clothes racks, waiting for someone who looked like they would buy the whole store. The employees were afraid that if they helped some of these cruise customers, the resulting purchase might only have one measly item, and that would hurt their *Items per Transaction* and *Average Sale* stat."

"You haven't been to our store lately, have you, Coach?" I ask incredulously. "You've just explained our store to a T. How did you know what it was like?"

"You're not alone," Coach reassures me. "Most companies fall into a similar trap, achieving local optimization while suffering as a whole."

The Profit Equation

"So what is the solution?" Samantha asks.

"Well, for starters, everyone has to be measured and rewarded on the whole equation, not just on his or her part. Each person needs to understand how he contributes in the conversion process and then help drive toward the final goal. Take *The Profit Equation*, for example."

$$\text{Customers} \times \frac{\text{Transactions}}{\text{Customers}} \times \frac{\text{Items}}{\text{Transactions}} \times \frac{\text{Sales}}{\text{Items}} \times \frac{\text{Profit}}{\text{Sales}} = \text{Profit}$$

"If marketing is measured on the whole equation—with an understanding that the marketing department has the greatest ability to influence the number of *Customers* piece of the equation—it would likely be more selective in the promotions it ran. It would focus its efforts on driving customers to the store who would likely become buyers and would likely purchase more. It might run a promotion that gave customers who purchased over $100 the opportunity to qualify for a trip to the Final Four. It may use the subequation for *Customers* we wrote on the board, but it will only use the subequation within the context of the whole equation. Marketing will understand that the cost of the promotion flows through to the profit of the company. Therefore, it will do the best it can to balance that against its role of bringing in new customers."

Coach stops for a minute to let us think.

"When you begin to shift toward local optimization, you inevitably hurt the whole. If you think about the sales staff again for a minute, there are other problems that could result from them just being focused on *Average Sale*. We already mentioned that they become selective in who they sell to, resulting in fewer transactions. The other risk you run is that people actually get too aggressive; they try too hard to sell to every single customer and push, push, push until they actually begin to make customers shy away from the store. In this case, you hurt the *Customers* piece of the equation."

"So," Samantha adds, "it sounds like the key is to balance all of the pieces. How does this work if not everyone has control over all of the pieces? It seems like people would naturally gravitate toward their areas of influence, ultimately causing the local optimization problem."

"You're right," Coach says. "That is the natural tendency. That's where a good leader becomes so essential. He has to have a perfectly clear vision of the whole picture. He can then keep the multiple pieces in check. He becomes the director who makes sure all of the pieces of the puzzle come together correctly."

"Sounds like quite a job." I can't help but think about Jimmy and the time and effort he puts in at the store.

"It is at first." Coach nods. "Once the leader understands the whole equation and is able to pass on the vision to his employees, it actually makes his job a lot easier. With everyone—even across different areas of the business—working on the same page toward the same goal, each individual understands his role, and there are a lot fewer fires to put out. The leader can then turn his full attention to managing the equation and removing roadblocks for his employees as they attempt to maximize the overall result."

"So, Coach," I say, "what's next?"

"Why don't you spend a little time trying to figure out what level of complexity will be most suitable for your given equation?"

"Wouldn't it be easier if you just told us, Coach?" I ask; I'm always looking for a quick answer.

"Well, like I said before, there's really no one correct answer. The key is to figure out how to expand and contract your equation so you can find the right equation for the given audience." Coach smiles as he erases the board. Then he starts writing up his lesson for first period.

"Okay." Samantha stands up and gets ready to go. "We'll see what we can do."

CHAPTER 18

We have a few minutes before class starts, and Samantha and I make our way over to the lockers near the commons area.

"So, what do you think?" I ask as Samantha spins the combination on her locker.

"We should probably look back through the variables and determine if any of the other variables we didn't use can be substituted to add value to what we have."

"That sounds reasonable," I agree. "One thing I thought about as we talked is that, for Jimmy, there's probably value in seeing what our costs are, so we can manage them; but I'm not exactly sure how we go about adding costs into the equation that we already have."

"I don't think it should be that hard," Samantha says. "Maybe we need to make a subequation. Something like this."

She takes my notebook and scribbles a new equation.

"The equation for *Profit* could also be written like this," Samantha says as she hands the notebook back.

$$\text{Sales} - \text{Costs} = \text{Profit}$$

"So can we just add that into our other equation in the place of *Profit* on the left-hand side of the equation?" I erase where *Profit* had been written and replace it with our new definition of *Profit*.

$$\text{Customers} \times \frac{\text{Transactions}}{\text{Customers}} \times \frac{\text{Items}}{\text{Transactions}} \times \frac{\text{Sales}}{\text{Items}} \times \frac{(\text{Sales} - \text{Costs})}{\text{Sales}} = \text{Profit}$$

I like it.

"I guess it's really just doing what Coach suggested about tweaking the equation until you find the right balance of complexity and simplicity that helps you drive the right behavior. Maybe as time goes on, we will end up simplifying some pieces and breaking down others until we get to the best answer."

"Yeah, I think you're right," Samantha says. "I imagine the closer you are to the actual workings of the equation, the more qualified and capable you are to make the necessary tweaks."

At that, the first bell rings, and we head down the hall—me toward English, and Samantha toward chemistry.

I imagine the first three periods of the day will crawl by as I wait for algebra. I wonder what we'll talk about today. Surprisingly, now that I have a real use for algebra, each class seems to have some application to the equations we are trying to build. I guess I've even started to look at everything that happens now in a little different light, trying to better understand how this process of equation building might apply across the various aspects of my life.

My thoughts turn to my date with Samantha on Saturday. I still can't believe that she actually said yes. I looked at the movies that are playing and don't know if any are really first-date worthy. Maybe we could go bowling or something.

I'm really not a kid who goes on a lot of dates. I just can't bring myself to believe that any girl would want to hang out with me. Slim always tells me that I shouldn't worry so much about it and that I should just have some fun, but I don't think that's how my brain functions.

Mrs. Anderson is droning on about some book that we are supposed to be reading. Between the time I've been spending with Samantha, basketball, and work, I haven't had time for much else. I know I've got to stay on top of things—or at least fake it—so I can stay eligible to play basketball.

Finally, algebra rolls around. Coach starts working through last night's homework equations. I didn't really have any questions about them, so I decide to see if I can build an equation for our basketball team. I pull out my notebook and flip to the next page.

The Profit Equation

Let's see. We proved last week against Hillcrest that the single number we should shoot for is *Total Points* scored. That seems pretty logical, and Coach said that, at the end of the day, the final answer has to be the one thing that you can't live without.

I guess the next step is to identify all of the potential pieces to my puzzle. I start to write:

Shooting Percentage
Rebounds
Steals
Points per Player

Let's see what kind of an equation I can build out of these. I start with *Total Points* on the right side.

$$= \text{Total Points}$$

The only other piece I have that includes points is *Points per Player*, so I add that to my equation and multiply it by *Players* so I get to my final result.

$$\text{Players} \times \frac{\text{Total Points}}{\text{Players}} = \text{Total Points}$$

So with 9 players on the team, if we could average 7 points per player each game, we should be able to score 63 points every night. I'm pretty sure that isn't the whole thing. I sit back and think about Coach's advice to break down the equation into more detail for better understanding. This equation is correct; it's just not descriptive enough to be very useful.

I'm pretty sure I can't get any more granular on *Players*. What about *Points per Player*? I think *Shooting Percentage* should fit into the equation somehow and definitely impacts *Points per Player*. I start to write again.

$$\text{Players} \times \frac{\text{Total Points}}{\text{Players}} \times \frac{\text{Shots Made}}{\text{Shots Taken}} = \text{Total Points}$$

Michael D. Batt

Well, that doesn't work. So what if I try to change the equation?

$$\text{Players} \times \frac{\text{Shots Taken}}{\text{Players}} \times \frac{\text{Shots Made}}{\text{Shots Taken}} = \text{Total Points}$$

I'm almost there. One more change, and it should be good.

$$\text{Players} \times \frac{\text{Shots Taken}}{\text{Players}} \times \frac{\text{Shots Made}}{\text{Shots Taken}} \times \frac{\text{Total Points}}{\text{Shots Made}} = \text{Total Points}$$

So that's it, huh? That was a lot easier to come up with than my first equation. I wonder what I'm missing. What about steals and rebounds? Do I have all of the pieces I need to make the equation complete?

I think through each piece of the equation. *Players*—that one's easy. Unfortunately, we can't add any more players to our roster—league rules. If we could add more players than the other team, we could definitely outrun teams with a constant set of fresh legs on the floor. I wonder if *Players* is the right first piece. The equation works, but in the store equation, the first piece is something we can expand, namely *Customers*. *Players* seem to be too restricted.

Next is *Shots Taken per Player*. I guess that just measures how many shots we are able to take through the course of the game. I guess steals and rebounds come into play there indirectly. If we can steal the ball or get rebounds, we increase the number of shots we can take in a set amount of time.

As I think about it, when we steal the ball or get a rebound, we are really just increasing the number of possessions that we have in the game. Maybe instead of players, I need to have possessions. That would fix my problem of having a first piece that is fixed instead of expandable.

I erase the first part of the equation and make the change.

$$\text{Possessions} \times \frac{\text{Shots Taken}}{\text{Possessions}} \times \frac{\text{Shots Made}}{\text{Shots Taken}} \times \frac{\text{Total Points}}{\text{Shots Made}} = \text{Total Points}$$

The Profit Equation

Beautiful. If we can increase the number of possessions we have in the game by forcing turnovers and playing tough defense, we will be able to take more shots, make more shots, and ultimately, get more points.

Moving on to the next piece of the equation, we have *Shots Made per Shots Taken*—Wally's beloved shooting percentage. Obviously, within the context of the whole equation, this is a valuable piece.

Last is *Points per Shots Made*. If we can get Slim to catch fire out in three-point land the value of each shot made will increase, driving up our total score.

Just like in the store, there are tradeoffs between the different pieces; you can't have it all. If we decide to pursue the *Points per Shot Made* piece by taking lots of three-pointers, our *Shots Made per Shots Taken* may suffer. If we are successful, though, we can get enough points to offset the decline in our shooting percentage.

Overall, I think this is great. The key will be to get the team to focus on the whole and not get caught up in the pieces. If we can tailor our strategy based on this equation and based on the team we are playing, I think we can really duplicate what happened last week against Hillcrest.

I guess the second part of the game is to understand that our opponents are working with the exact same equation, and we need to control their outcome. Tough defense will limit the number of their possessions, drive down their shooting percentage, limit the number of three-pointers that they shoot.... Success will only come as we drive our equation and work on restricting theirs.

I guess it is the same for the store. At the store, we are really just competing for our customers' limited disposable incomes. They come to the mall with a $100, and it is our job to convince them—through good selection, good service, etc—to spend their money with us instead of at another store.

Interesting. The process is really, very similar.

Coach told us upfront that it wouldn't be too hard once we figured it out. I guess he was right.

Chapter 19

The bell rings, and the class starts to file toward the door. I don't really have plans for lunch but I was hoping to talk with Samantha about what I've been working on the past couple of hours.

"Davis." Coach catches me. "Can we talk a minute?"

I set my bag down on a chair in the back of the room and head up to Coach's desk, where he is straightening the assignments we just turned in.

"What's up, Coach?" I ask.

"Not much. I just noticed you weren't with us today in class. I thought about sending an eraser your way, but I figured you were probably thinking through your equation. Let's see what you've come up with."

"Well, on my work equation, Samantha made a nice addition. I mentioned as we left your room this morning that it would be nice to see the costs of running the store broken out. She made another equation for *Profit* and then substituted it in for where we had *Profit* on the left-hand side of our equation."

I hand my notebook to Coach so he can check it out.

$$\text{Customers} \times \frac{\text{Transactions}}{\text{Customers}} \times \frac{\text{Items}}{\text{Transactions}} \times \frac{\text{Sales}}{\text{Items}} \times \frac{(\text{Sales} - \text{Costs})}{\text{Sales}} = \text{Profit}$$

"What do you think?" I ask as Coach looks at my scribbling.

"I like it." Coach smiles. "I think that is a good change. Let me ask you a follow-up question. What if Jimmy says that he wants

The Profit Equation

to view different costs separately? For example, he wants to see *Cost of Goods*—the cost of the products you sell—independent from *Rent, Utilities, Wages*—the operating expenses. How might you change your equation to accommodate this request?"

I wish Samantha were here, for more reasons than one. She came up with this change in the first place and would probably know what to do. I sit down and stare at my equation.

"Can I just break those costs out in the last part of the equation like this?"

$$\frac{\text{Sales} - \text{Cost of Goods} - \text{Rent} - \text{Utilities} - \text{Labor}\ldots}{\text{Sales}}$$

"Exactly." Coach smiles. "Let me show you one more way you can show it as well. Remember that, if the figure on the bottom is the same for two fractions, you can subtract those from each other. You can use that principle in reverse to change your equation like this."

$$\frac{\text{Sales}}{\text{Sales}} - \frac{\text{Cost of Goods}}{\text{Sales}} - \frac{\text{Rent}}{\text{Sales}} - \frac{\text{Utilities}}{\text{Sales}} - \frac{\text{Labor}}{\text{Sales}} \ldots$$

"Now Jimmy can evaluate as a percentage of sales how the expenses breakdown. He might find that *Cost of Goods* is 45 percent, *Rent* is 12 percent, *Wages* are 6 percent, etc. You can then compare these percentages over time to determine where you are trending."

"I guess you can then focus on decreasing each of them in turn to help maximize your profit," I interject.

"Not so quick," Coach says. "You may actually determine that *increasing* some of your expenses will help you drive your overall profitability. For example, you may find that bringing in goods that have slightly higher *Cost of Goods* in relation to what you sell them for will drive your *Total Customers* or increase your number of *Transactions per Customer*. Remember, the goal is never to optimize a single piece of the equation. The pieces are only useful in helping you maximize the whole."

"Oh, that's right," I say, remembering. "So how do you not end up overanalyzing everything in fear that a change to one piece won't negatively impact another?"

"That's definitely a risk, Davis," Coach says. "The key is to do your best. If you are at least conscious of the interdependency of the multiple pieces and move forward accordingly, pretty quickly, you'll gain a good understanding of what might happen if you make a change to any given piece."

"What if you end up guessing wrong?" I ask.

"I can guarantee that occasionally you'll guess wrong." Coach says. "I can, however, promise you that, if you are at least asking the questions about how this decision might impact the other pieces of the puzzle—and ultimately the whole—you'll find that your mistakes won't be nearly as serious. Once you make a decision, you can monitor all of the other pieces and see what happens. You'll learn a lot through the process."

"I think I've already learned a ton, Coach," I say. "Samantha and I decided that it's going to take some time to tweak our equation, but I think I understand now some of the different ways I can do it. Once we identify our ideal equation, Coach, what should we do next?"

"That's the golden question, Davis." Coach sits down next to me. "I've tried to teach these principles to lots of people. I think most get it, but at the end of the day, it really only helps a few."

"Why's that?" I wonder out loud. "I don't see how someone could get the principle and not be helped by it."

"Knowing is only half the battle."

"What's the other half?" I ask.

"Application and execution," Coach answers unequivocally. "A lot of people get it and then go on living and acting unchanged. Many even profess to apply it, but a closer look reveals that they are still measuring around individual pieces and only obtaining local optimization. It's hard to change what you've done for years, especially if you've experienced some degree of success. All too often, people sacrifice the best for the good."

The Profit Equation

"So how do you apply and execute based on an equation?" I'm hoping Coach can give me some good advice in preparation for my discussion with the team tonight and Jimmy tomorrow.

"There's no single right way to drive an equation, Davis. Two people may have the exact same equation but completely different strategies. Let me give you an example. Consider your equation."

$$\text{Customers} \times \frac{\text{Transactions}}{\text{Customers}} \times \frac{\text{Items}}{\text{Transactions}} \times \frac{\text{Sales}}{\text{Items}} \times \frac{(\text{Sales} - \text{Costs})}{\text{Sales}} = \text{Profit}$$

"This same equation applies to most retailers within the mall. One retailer may decide that they are going to pay for a premier spot—so their rent is through the roof—in order to get a lot of foot traffic. They may focus on selling high-end jewelry and have a relatively low number of *Transactions per Customer* and *Items Sold per Transaction* but a very high *Sales per Items Sold*.

"Another retailer right across the hall may be paying the same rent and getting the same foot traffic but offer inexpensive items with the hope of having a high volume of *Transactions per Customer* and a high number of *Items Sold per Transaction*."

"So which store is right?" I ask.

"They're both right, Davis," Coach says. "As long as they are staying true to their strategy and execution of it, they can both be successful. The problem comes when the high volume, low price store decides that they should start to measure *Average Sale*. They then bring in more expensive items and hope to maintain their high conversion rate. They quickly find that, as they drive up their *Average Sale*, their overall *Profit* begins to suffer. They don't get it, because the two figures should be connected. The problem is they are spending too much time looking across the hall, trying to figure out how to drive up their *Average Sale* like the jewelry store, not understanding that the key to the jewelry store's success is different than their own."

"What can a company do then to make sure it doesn't fall into this trap?" I wonder. I'm full of questions now on the application half of the process.

"I think there are two basic principles that will guide them. First, they have to understand their equation and how it works; that's always the first principle. Second, they need to set bounds within which they operate. Every equation has to have boundaries."

"I don't know that I follow you, Coach." I scratch my head and lean back in my chair. "What do you mean by boundaries?"

"Well, think about your basketball team, Davis. Your goal is to score more points than the other team, right?"

"Right."

"So why don't you put a couple of big guys like Slim down under the hoop and tell them that anytime somebody gets within ten feet of the basket to level 'em?"

"They'd be on the bench in no time, and we'd be out of big men."

"So get more big men," Coach counters. "Have twenty guys on your bench with that specific job."

"You know we can only have nine guys on the team. Otherwise, it would be a great strategy," I say.

"So there are rules that dictate your conduct on the court. They are established to ensure a fair, safe game."

"Sure, but I don't think there are any rules like that for our store," I argue.

"Well, just a minute," Coach says. "You could probably make a lot of money if you started selling drugs from the store or alcohol to minors. But obviously, that would be against the law."

"Okay, so there are laws that we have to abide by. But that doesn't keep us from purchasing more expensive items or trying to increase our average order."

"You're right," Coach says. "That is where a company has to establish its own rules. Sometimes, they do it by way of a mission statement or a set of values. Just like a basketball court has an out-of-bounds, a company has to set its own boundaries, in many cases. They have to decide what they are and what they aren't. They have to determine in what ways they will pursue profits and in what ways they won't. Then they have to have the discipline to stay within the bounds they have set."

"Are there ever instances when they can change the boundaries?" I ask.

"Sure," Coach says. "But they have to be careful. I've seen way too many cases when a team, a company, or an organization lets the mission constantly change until they don't appear to have any boundaries at all. They don't play their game, execute their strategy, and operate within their equation. They end up trying to match others' execution of the equation and inevitably are in trouble. It's just something to be aware of."

Coach stops for a minute to let me think about that. A company has to set boundaries. At work, we're a sports store. That's what we do. We're not a lotion store or a game store or any other kind of store, for that matter—even if a lot of other companies make money selling those things. We have to identify what we are and stick to it.

Finally, Coach interrupts my thoughts and continues.

"Let's get back to your original question about the second half of the process—the application and execution. Once you know what your equation is and how the pieces work together, you identify your boundaries—whether set by an outside force like a referee or the law or set by yourself to keep you true to what you are. Once you've done that, you are ready to really get into the guts of applying and executing according to your equation."

"So what's the first step?" I ask. "I'm not even sure how to start."

"That's a great question. I think a lot of people don't start, because they're not sure how. Honestly, it probably doesn't matter where you start, as long as you do. It's really an ongoing process that'll take some time. The key is to always come back and focus on the activities that will drive the conversion from one piece to the next."

"What do you mean by focus on the activities that will drive the conversion? I'm not sure I'm following you."

"Well, think about your equation," Coach says. "What will convert a customer into a buyer or a transaction?"

"If he can find what he wants, I guess."

"Okay, so how does he find what he wants?" Coach pushes me on.

"Well, we have to have that specific item for starters, and then a lot of times, there has to be someone to help him find it."

"Great." Coach seems happy enough with my response. "So what will make that happen?"

"I guess we need to communicate to our inventory purchasers what types of things people are in the store looking for, and then we need to get out from behind the counter and actually help people when they come in the store."

"Exactly." Coach grins and pats me on the knee. "So that is the first step. You start there, and then you go to the next conversion that needs to take place and ask the same question. What will convert my buyer from a buyer of one item into a buyer of multiple items, increasing my *Items per Transaction?*"

I look again at my equation.

$$\text{Customers} \times \frac{\text{Transactions}}{\text{Customers}} \times \frac{\text{Items}}{\text{Transactions}} \times \frac{\text{Sales}}{\text{Items}} \times \frac{(\text{Sales} - \text{Costs})}{\text{Sales}} = \text{Profit}$$

"Anytime you have a multiplication symbol in your equation," Coach continues, "you are going to go through this conversion process. When you see the multiplication symbol, ask yourself 'What do I need to do to make this conversion happen as seamlessly as possible?' Remember also, that you always need to keep in the back of your mind what effect the decisions you make might have on other pieces of the equation.

"The companies and teams that can master this process are the ones that will succeed. They focus on the end result—in this case, *Profit*—and then they work relentlessly to understand and drive the conversions that will help them get to that end result."

I look up at the clock and realize that the lunch hour is almost over. I still have a bunch of questions, but I know that

Coach probably needs to grab a bite to eat and get ready for his next class.

"Sorry, I've kept you from getting lunch, Coach. I sure appreciate you walking me through these next steps. I think I've got an idea of what I should do next."

"It may sound a little complicated at first, but once you get rolling, it will be just like building equations; it comes pretty naturally!" Coach stands up and begins to erase the board.

"So, Davis," Coach says without turning around. "I remember when we first started talking, you mentioned that you had three problems—your work, your basketball team, and your girl situation. We've spent a good amount of time working on your job equation but haven't talked much about the other two. It looks like you and Samantha are spending a good amount of time together. Have you put much thought into building any other equations?"

"Not too much," I admit. "I was working a little bit on our basketball team's equation 'cause Slim's been bugging me about it, and we have our next big game later this week. I also have a date with Samantha this week, so even though I haven't thought about the girl equation, things seem to be going good there. I think the learning curve won't be too steep as I start to work on the others."

"I think you're right. The process is the same; it's just the pieces that are different. Remember that, even if things are going well—like with Samantha—it never hurts to build an equation to help you keep things on track. The difference between goodness and greatness often lies in going through the motions of mapping out your plan."

"Thanks for the reminder, Coach." I stand up and put my papers in my bag. "I'll keep that in mind."

Michael D. Batt

CHAPTER 20

As Spanish gets underway, I retrace my conversation with Coach. We reviewed expanding and contracting equations, and then we discussed the application of the equation. We started with boundaries and then we focused on the activities that drive conversion. Coach said that each multiplication symbol represents an activity that will drive conversion to the next level.

Now that I'm an expert at building equations, maybe I'll try to build an equation for my girl problem and see how it goes. If my goal is to get a girlfriend, what things might I measure? I start to make a list.

      Girls I know
      Girls I have asked out
      Girls I've asked out more than once
      Girls I've held hands with

I guess at some point I have to determine what constitutes a girlfriend. Otherwise, I may not ever know when I've arrived. I think about it for a minute and determine that, if I kiss a girl, that should be sufficient to signify that we are boyfriend and girlfriend. I add that to the end of my list.

I start putting the pieces together. It's definitely getting easier than the first time I tried to build one of these equations.

The Profit Equation

$$\text{Girls I know} \times \frac{\text{Girls asked out}}{\text{Girls I know}} \times \frac{\text{Girls asked out} > 1 \text{ time}}{\text{Girls asked out}} \times \frac{\text{Girls held hands with}}{\text{Girls asked out} > 1 \text{ time}} \times \frac{\text{Girls kissed}}{\text{Girls held hands with}} = \text{Girls kissed}$$

As the teacher drones on in Spanish, I look at my equation and begin to feel a little concerned. If the starting point is *Girls I Know*, I'm doomed. Despite the fact that I play on the varsity basketball team, I'm shy enough that I don't really know that many girls.

I decide to take my equation back one more step.

$$\text{Girls in School} \times \frac{\text{Girls I know}}{\text{Girls in school}} \times \frac{\text{Girls asked out}}{\text{Girls I know}} \times \frac{\text{Girls asked out} > 1 \text{ time}}{\text{Girls asked out}} \times \frac{\text{Girls held hands with}}{\text{Girls asked out} > 1 \text{ time}} \times \frac{\text{Girls kissed}}{\text{Girls held hands with}} = \text{Girls kissed}$$

Okay. That seems more like it. I don't really know what the boundaries are, so maybe I'll try to list out the activities that drive conversion, and then I'll come back to the boundaries later. First off, I need to figure out how to change more of the girls in our school into girls that I know.

What activities would make that happen? I guess I'd need to actually go to some of the school dances—as much as I hate them. What else? It seems like some guys have all the luck with the girls. What do they do?

They talk to girls. They're involved with groups that girls are involved with as well. They hang out with other guys who have girls around them …

So, if Samantha ends up dogging me and I have to start at square one, the first thing I need to do is start getting to know more girls. The more girls I know, the bigger the pool of girls who could potentially be converted into girls I could ask out.

I guess the next conversion is easy—at least conceptually. To change a girl that I know into a girl that I have asked out, I need to actually ask her out. No wonder Coach said some people understand the logic of equations but don't put them into practice. I sure have a hard time asking girls out.

If I really want to get to my end result, I imagine there will be other difficult choices to make. I can only imagine that kissing a girl might be a little more nerve-racking than asking her out.

No problem. *Right*, I think sarcastically.

I guess I need to take one step at a time. It doesn't seem too daunting to get to know more girls. I just need to put myself in situations where I can meet more girls.

I can see now what Coach means about focusing on the activities that drive the conversion from one piece to the next. If I can keep the end goal in mind and then work on the pieces in that context, I think even shy Andy Davis could kiss a girl … eventually.

I sit back and laugh to myself about what I've just done. I'm sure Samantha would die to think I'd just built an equation for kissing her! We'll have to see how it works.

Anyway, back to the task at hand. *If I take the same concept and apply it to my other equations …*

I spend the rest of Spanish trying to figure out what activities will drive conversion in my first two equations—work and basketball. I realize as I go that, in many cases, the same activity drives multiple conversions.

For example, at work, if we can improve our product selection, we can convert more customers into buyers and, at the same time, potentially drive up the *Items per Transaction*. As word gets out that our selection has improved, it may ultimately drive up our customer count as well.

I'd be willing to bet that some of the activities that drive multiple conversions would be a good place to focus our initial efforts.

By the time Spanish is over, I have a page for each equation that maps out the activities that drive conversion. With our basketball team equation, for example, I have added a column of activities under each point of conversion. I started with a column to describe ways to get more possessions.

The Profit Equation

$$\text{Possessions} \times \frac{\text{Shots Taken}}{\text{Possessions}} \times \frac{\text{Shots Made}}{\text{Shots Taken}} \times \frac{\text{Total Points}}{\text{Shots Made}} = \text{Total Points}$$

Activities	Activities	Activities	Activities
Tough defense	Good plays	Look for open man	3 pointers
Rebounds	Watch shot clock	Smart shots	Setting screens
Steals	Setting screens	Good plays	Good passes
Hustling	Good passes	Setting screens	
		Good passes	

Michael D. Batt

I'm sure this isn't a complete list, but at least it's a start. As we play as a team, we can decide which activities drive which conversions most effectively. I hope that then we can focus our efforts. At first glance, it is obvious that making good clean passes, setting screens, and having good plays will help us drive multiple conversions. While these appear to be no-brainers, I think as we execute them with the clear intent to drive conversion from one piece to the next, the "Why" behind the activity will help us do it with a little more heart.

I think we will also find that this will clarify the real value of a statistic like shooting percentage. We will better understand that a good shooting percentage is only valuable if the rest of the pieces of the puzzle are coming together. If we sacrifice the other pieces for the sake of shooting percentage, the end result—*Total Points*—will suffer. If we can keep focused on *Total Points*, we should have a more balanced attack on each of the pieces. So, what next?

As I sit through art and then head to the gym for basketball practice, I mull over the best way to get buy-in for this new way of thinking. I'm the captain of the team, but Wally is still the coach. At work, I'm just a lowly hourly employee. I know that, for this to really work, it has to come from the top.

I get dressed and head out to the court to start warming up with the other guys. It only takes Slim about thirty seconds to come over and interrupt my stretching routine.

"So what's the plan, Davis?"

Slim is all business when it comes to winning. He'd give his left arm for a state championship, but until lately, he'd about given up on the idea.

"I think I've got a plan. The question is how we should go about executing it."

I'll be honest. I haven't figured it out yet.

"Well, I talked to Wally a few minutes ago and told him you've been working on something with Coach H. He's nearly a legend around here, you know, taking our ragamuffin baseball team all the way to state last year. I think you have Wally's ear if this stuff is coming from Coach H."

The Profit Equation

That may be just the break I need.

"Well, why don't you let me finish stretching and go ask Wally if we can have a little team meeting before we practice? Maybe Charley can grab the whiteboard in the locker room, and we can make this official."

My mind starts to race as I try to formulate a plan on how to lay this process out so it makes sense. I decide that my best strategy will be to walk the team through the equation I worked on today during class and then talk to them about boundaries and the activities that drive conversion.

I finish stretching and join a group of the guys. They are shooting around while we wait for Charley to come back with the whiteboard. We've got a pretty good group of guys, and I think they'll get it. They all want to win, but we've just been missing a vital piece that has kept us from coming through on our desire. I think I've got the missing link.

Charley finally makes his way up the ramp from the locker room, whiteboard in tow. Wally calls the team over to the bleachers and begins practice by congratulating us on our big win against Hillcrest last week. He then talks for a few minutes about our game this Friday night against Skyline.

Skyline creamed us two weeks ago, so everyone is a little skittish about playing them again. Wally gives us a little pep talk about how we were just off the last game and had a lower than average shooting percentage. He reassures us that if we can change a few things this week, he's confident we can win.

Finally, it's my turn. Wally tells the team I've got something to share that I think can help us come together as a team. He sits down, and it's all me.

I start with a question: "So, who thinks we have a shot this week against Skyline?"

Whether from confidence or from fear that Wally will think they don't have faith in the team, everyone raises his hand. I'm pretty sure that at least a few of the guys, including Slim, have their doubts.

"What's it going to take to win this game?" I ask.

"A good shooting percentage," Charley says.

"Okay." I'll go along with that for now. "What else?"

"Good defense," Slim suggests. "They have a good inside game, so we'll need to be tough on shutting down the lanes and grabbing the boards—offensive and defensive."

"Sure. Any other thoughts?" I ask. We sit silently for a few moments, and then I go on. "So let's say that we play tough defense and keep Skyline to 40 points on the night."

"That'd be a miracle," someone mutters under his breath, confirming my suspicion that not everyone is completely confident we can pull this off.

"Now let's assume that Skyline only scores 40 points and we shoot 75 percent from the field," I say. "Would we win the game?"

"Of course, we would," Wally says. "If you guys can shoot 75 percent on Friday night, I'll take the whole team to dinner afterward."

"Are you sure about that, Wally?"

"No doubt!" Wally is confident.

"So, what if now that you have offered to take us to dinner if we can shoot 75 percent, we get so gun-shy and wait all night for perfect shots. Say we only shoot 20 shots and they are all inside layups that we can't miss. We hit 16—so 80 percent of our shots. The rest of our possessions result in the other team stealing the ball or some sort of an error on our part that results in a turnover. We end the night with 32 points; we hold Skyline to 40 points and shoot over 75 percent; and we still lose the game."

"Are you serious, Davis?" Wally seems a little annoyed that I'd even suggest that we'd only shoot 20 shots in a night.

"Sure." I smile. "Slim will do almost anything for a free dinner. You don't think we won the game last week without Slim getting a meal out of the deal, do you? I know my example is an extreme case, but you have to admit that it could happen. We could play tough defense, have a great shooting percentage, and still lose the game."

The Profit Equation

"Okay, I get your point." Wally seems to soften a little. "So, what do you think we should do? How do we take this scenario you just gave us and make it a defining factor in our game Friday night?"

Here goes nothing, I think. I pull the whiteboard over and write the equation on the board.

$$\text{Possessions} \times \frac{\text{Shots Taken}}{\text{Possessions}} \times \frac{\text{Shots Made}}{\text{Shots Taken}} \times \frac{\text{Total Points}}{\text{Shots Made}} = \text{Total Points}$$

When I'm done, I step back and give everyone a chance to look over the equation. After a minute or so, I turn back to the board and circle "Shots Made / Shots Taken."

"This is our shooting percentage. It's a critical piece of the puzzle, but it's only a piece. If we are going to win games, we have to maximize the whole and not get lost in the pieces. I admit that the example I just talked through is not very realistic. But I think the concept is sound. If we can take a step back and understand how everything that we do—from what we eat for breakfast to what we do in practice to how we play on the floor—ultimately impacts this equation, we can start to consistently come up with some wins."

"So what does that mean we need to do differently?" Slim asks. "Do we need to practice differently or eat something different for breakfast? I guess I don't see how this equation will change what we do."

I'm glad he asked the question. "Great point, Slim. The question really is 'How will we change?'"

I walk the team through the concept of conversion and how it applies to the equation, ultimately changing possessions into total points scored. I then go to the board and write "Activities" under each multiplication symbol, similar to the page I wrote in Spanish this afternoon. Slim's question is a great segue into talking about activities that drive conversion. I know I had planned to talk about boundaries first, but I'll have to come back to that.

I walk the team through the activities that potentially drive conversion from one piece of the equation to the next. We list a lot of the same answers that I had already listed, but the team comes up with some great ideas that I hadn't written down earlier.

When we're done listing the activities, I ask how this diagram might change the way we as a team can approach our practices and games.

Charley speaks first. "I think if we understand the role of each of these activities in driving the conversions—as you call them—we can hopefully pay more attention to how we practice them and how diligent we are in the mastery of the different skills."

"I think we can also use the equation to plan specifically for each opponent we may play," Slim says. "We may need to focus on one area of the equation when we play Hillcrest and another area of the equation when we play Skyline. No more cookie-cutter playing where shooting percentage is the only dictating metric. We can have a more balanced attack."

"Alright, Slim," Wally says. He's still not completely sold. I guess when you've played and taught a certain principle—such as shooting percentage—your whole life, you don't change in an afternoon. "Given what you just said, how would you suggest we approach our game this weekend against Skyline? I'm having a hard time seeing how we would ever develop a strategy where shooting percentage wouldn't be of utmost importance."

"Well, Wally," Slim is careful as he picks his words. "Like I said a few minutes ago, Skyline has a great inside game. They have some solid, big men who make penetration tough. Last time we played them, we kept going inside, mainly because it's a lot easier to get a high shooting percentage shooting layups than it is shooting threes. Davis was having a great night that night from beyond the arch, but great is all relative. If you shoot 50 percent from the three-point line, it's considered great. If we shoot like that overall, you'd be all over us the next week in practice.

"I guess my point is, maybe we need to design our game plan around Skyline specifically. We need to come out early shooting threes, understanding that our shooting percentage will

The Profit Equation

suffer. Hopefully, we make it up in the extra *Points per Shot Made*." Slim points at that part of the equation before he continues. "In addition, hopefully we can open up the inside and create opportunities for an inside game later on in the game. Last week when we played Hillcrest, I think it was just the opposite. They have some great guards who make shooting from the perimeter a little tougher. We were able to penetrate early on and get their guards to pull in, giving us the opportunity to shoot more outside later on in the game. It really just worked out that way. If we could make that conscious decision and plan going into our games each week, I think we would be much more successful in our attempt to win."

The guys sit quietly for a few minutes, letting Slim's comments sink in and giving Wally a chance to digest this new way of thinking.

Finally, Wally breaks the silence. "I think I can go along with this and give it a try. I do think we need to get a little deeper though. Let's talk for a minute about reasons that we aren't doing some of these things? Like why don't we hustle, why do we not execute plays well, why do we force shots? My gut tells me we are missing some of the root reasons behind the activities. Let's start with why we don't execute plays? What do you guys think? Why don't they work?"

I decide I can give a reasonable answer to that one. "I think we don't know which plays to run when. We force plays in situations or against teams that just don't fit. I'm also not sure that we've quite mastered the plays in the first place. Maybe if we knew the plays by heart and we knew when we should run each play, we would be better prepared to execute them more effectively."

Wally nods his agreement.

"So what you're saying is that when we are working on plays during practice, there shouldn't be quite so much moaning and griping and a little more focus? I guess I also need to spend a little more time talking through what situations call for what plays."

It's true. We'd much rather scrimmage than work on Wally's crazy plays and drills. Usually, the portion of practice when we are running through plays ends with frustration on Wally's part, and he tells us to scrimmage for a while and then hit the showers.

"That's probably true," I agree with Wally. "I wonder too if our plays are a little too complicated sometimes. Halfway through the play someone forgets where he's supposed to be, and the play falls apart."

"I can live with that," Wally says. "If you guys can master some of the basic plays and learn to execute them perfectly, I think we would be fine."

Everyone nods agreement.

"So what about hustling?" Wally moves on. "What keeps us from giving 100 percent day in and day out?"

The guys start to list off a couple of reasons—staying up too late the night before, poor conditioning, etc.

After we list a bunch of reasons, Wally asks, "So in my mind, the question is 'How badly do you want to win?' Are you willing to do what it takes? Do we have the discipline to really pour over this equation and list of activities and commit ourselves to make it happen?"

Everyone nods.

"Davis." Wally turns to me. "As the captain, will you commit to make sure the guys are giving their all and call 'em out if they start to slack? As a coaching staff, we'll put some thought into each of the activities that we've listed and see what we can do to design our practices around mastering them."

"Sounds good, Wally." I think it's clicked with Wally. As I look around the room, I get the sense that everyone else is onboard as well.

"So what do we do today?" Slim asks. "We have to start somewhere, right?"

Everyone turns to Wally, waiting for our marching orders.

"Well, first of all, no more wasting practices scrimmaging. People always say practice makes perfect, but in reality, only perfect practice makes perfect. Any other kind of practice only makes things permanent."

A few people moan a little.

The Profit Equation

"Hey, guys," I remind them. "Remember, if we want to start winning consistently, we've got to do some things differently. We can't expect different results as long as we keep doing what we've been doing the last few months."

Even though everyone seems to get it, I'm sure it's going to take some time to get everyone fully up to speed and to see the value of the changes.

Wally is up now and rolling the ball rack out on the court.

"Okay, guys," he says. "Let's get going. We'll start with our passing drills. Remember: perfect practice makes perfect."

Instead of just letting us go through the motions like we usually do, Wally stops us several times and corrects our mistakes. As we run through the drills, Wally walks us through the importance of making crisp, clean passes—the "Why" that makes us realize that good passes really are essential to getting good open shots, which ultimately improves our likelihood of making shots.

After passing drills, we start to work on plays. About two minutes into the exercise, Slim makes a beautiful behind-the-back pass to me as I cut through the lane for a layup. Wally blows the whistle and breaks up the play.

Wally grabs the ball from Slim and get's in his grill. "Slim, what's up with the behind-the-back pass? What did that get you that a simple bounce pass wouldn't?"

"I don't know, Coach." Slim shrugs his shoulders. "Everybody does it."

"Everybody but us starting today. If we really want to make this work, we have to eliminate the risk of errors whenever it isn't necessary. Davis caught your pass, but what if there was another defender right behind you or what if Davis hadn't been looking? We have to play smart basketball. We didn't just spend thirty minutes running through passing drills for nothing! Let's run it again. This time nice and clean bounce passes."

We start over and run the drill again. Slim gets the ball at the top of the key and fakes left and then makes a bounce pass to me as I cut into the lane and make an easy layup.

"Perfect!" Wally smiles. "Now do it again. We'll run it 'til we can do it in our sleep."

We continue to practice that play and a few others for the next hour, and then Wally asks us to run laps around the top of the gym, coming up and down the stairs on every other lap.

Practice runs a little longer than usual, and we never get to scrimmage, but everyone seems okay with it. I'm surprised to see how good Wally is at setting up plays and running them until we get it right. I never knew; we never really spent much time working on them before.

There was a new sense of underlying purpose in practice today. It wasn't just to get to scrimmage; it was much more focused and intense. The goal of mastering the conversion activities—even just associating the different drills with the conversion concept—made all of our activities more meaningful.

Wally asked us to come in before school the next few days to get ready for our game against Skyline. If we are going to make this happen, he tells us, we need all the practice we can get.

As we hit the showers, everyone is tired but pleased with the way things went today.

"Davis," Slim catches up to me as I'm getting dressed. "I think we actually have a chance this week. If we can really come through and run this thing right, I think we have the talent to make it happen."

"I agree. We just have to be careful not to let anyone get too caught up on any one metric. Like last week, we need to stay focused on the whole—the total points scored—and then use the other stats as tools to help us drive the end result."

Slim ties his shoes.

"Well, you heard Wally. You're in charge of making sure we all stay on track." He pats me on the back as he stands to leave.

CHAPTER 21

As I pull up to her house, Samantha's out on the front steps working on her homework. She looks great! Samantha was a little upset when she found out that I spent lunch talking to Coach. I promised I'd catch her up to speed after practice tonight.

I'm excited to go out with her on Saturday; I only wish I didn't have to wait until then. As I get out of the car, I review in my mind my girlfriend equation. I guess, right now, I am at the point of conversion from *Girls Asked Out* to *Girls Asked Out More than Once*, since I've technically asked her out—even if we haven't actually gone out. So, what activities do I need to consider in order to move to the next piece?

I probably need to make sure the first date is a success. I think I can borrow my dad's Camaro, if I promise to be careful. I need to come up with some cash so I can take her out to dinner somewhere nice. I wonder what Samantha would classify as a successful date. I'm sure she goes out all the time, and I don't want to look like the cheap kid on the block.

There's probably a hundred other activities I could do to make the first date a success. I'm just not sure what they are.

Samantha looks up from her book as I walk up the sidewalk.

"Hi, Andy!"

"Hi, Samantha." I wave.

"How was practice?" Samantha asks.

"It was good. Sorry I'm a little late. Wally worked us over tonight. I've been dying to talk to you. Coach gave me some great insight today during lunch, and then we started to use it tonight at practice. I actually think it's going to work, Samantha."

"So, tell me what he told you," Samantha says. "I think we are pretty good at making equations now, but I'm not sure what we need to do next. I imagine that's what Coach talked to you about today, right?"

"Yeah. It seems so simple; I'm not sure why we didn't figure it out on our own, but I guess that could be said of the whole process. Once we get it, it seems pretty natural."

"That's true. So, come on, tell me what he said." Samantha is anxious to continue.

I tell her how Coach explained that application is the second half of the battle and how a lot of people don't ever get past it. We then talk about boundaries, and I tell her about Coach's example of our basketball team and having big men inside to take out anyone who tries to drive to the hoop.

Finally, I tell her about the activities that drive conversion. I think this is really the key to the process: trying to figure out which activities drive which conversions and then figuring out ways to really make the changes necessary so you are only doing the vital activities and not wasting time on nonessential activities.

Last but not least, I tell her about our basketball practice and how it all came together. She seems pretty impressed with how quickly Wally grasped the idea and ran with it. I agree that it was fun to watch and tell her that I'm excited to see what comes of it as we face Skyline on Friday.

As I finish talking, I realize I've completely monopolized the conversation to this point.

"So, what's next Andy? Where do we go from here? It sounds like your basketball team is on the right path. What about your work?"

"Well," I say, "I work again tomorrow night, so I'll go through this process with Jimmy and see if we can't get it rolling before he ends up in hot water with the DM because of slumping sales."

The Profit Equation

We sit and talk for a few minutes about trying to get people to buy into this new way of approaching problems. It appears that Wally is on board, and Jimmy should come along as well. It's really such a clear, simple way to think about things. You identify your end result, figure out the steps to get there, set boundaries, and then put the steps together like pieces of a puzzle, focusing on the activities that make everything come together.

There seem to be a couple of areas that we can think of that are potential pitfalls in helping other people adopt the new model. We jot them down so we can address them as we discuss the equations with other people. Assuming that people get through the process of building the equation, there are three problems.

1. People don't want to change. They hold fast to their old paradigms.
2. People still get too focused on the pieces instead of the ultimate goal. They get the process but can't let go of measuring and rewarding based on the pieces instead of the whole.
3. People get stuck within boundaries that only exist in their minds. They fail to get outside the box to really make the equation work.

The more we talk, the more excited I get about the potential of this new process. I think this will really change the way I function in life. Of course, like Coach said, I have to have the discipline to actually apply the process, but if I stick to it, I think it will help me with any problem I may have.

As we continue to talk, my thoughts switch back to our date this weekend. I wonder how I can figure out what Samantha considers a successful date. I could just ask her, but that seems a little weird. Maybe I'll ask my sister and see what things have impressed her.

I wonder if Samantha has siblings. I should probably know, but because we don't live in the same neighborhood, I just don't.

"So, Samantha," I change the topic unannounced. "I've met your dad and mom, but I haven't met the rest of your family. How many brothers and sisters do you have?"

"It's just me and an older brother, Tim. I think my parents would have liked a couple more kids, but it just never worked out."

"So what does Tim do?" I ask.

"He's almost six years older than me," Samantha says. "He moved out about four years ago to go to college. He'll be done in a year or two with his master's, and I don't know where he'll end up after that."

"Do you miss him?"

"Sure. Even though we are pretty far apart in age, he's always really looked out for me. It's been hard not having him around. He's studying engineering, and I don't know if there are many jobs around here that would bring him back."

"Is he married?"

"No." Samantha smiles. "I guess that's where we're kind of alike. Neither of us have ever been big daters. I think he'd like to be married and settle down, but he doesn't really know how to go about it."

I can hardly believe that Samantha doesn't go on a lot of dates. I think she's one of the cutest girls in school. She is kind of a bookworm, but I honestly thought she went out all the time, which is probably one of the reasons I've never asked her out before. Maybe it will make my date with her a little less stressful, knowing I'm not competing against all of her other dating experiences.

"Maybe we could make an equation for your brother's dating problem," I joke—kind of.

"That sounds like fun. Do you think it would really work for something like that?" Samantha asks.

"Sure." I grin. "I think it works for any kind of problem."

"Okay," she agrees. "Let's give it a try."

"Well, let's start by figuring out the end result," I say.

"What about marriage?" Samantha asks. "I think that's what he'd like."

"Sounds good."

Samantha starts the equation:

= Marriage

"I guess now we need to identify the pieces that will lead to *Marriage*."

We start to identify possible items to measure, while Samantha takes notes. I don't say much, but I throw out a few ideas that might be applicable pieces.

> Girls known
> Girls asked out
> Girls asked out more than once
> Girl held hands with
> Girls kissed
> Girlfriends
> Girls asked to marry
> Girls married

We build the equation without much problem. We decide that his universe of girls will be the girls at his school, similar to in my equation. We're pretty good at the process now, not to mention I've built this equation once before:

$$\text{Girls in School} \times \frac{\text{Girls known}}{\text{Girls in school}} \times \frac{\text{Girls asked out}}{\text{Girls known}} \times \frac{\text{Girls asked out} > 1 \text{ time}}{\text{Girls asked out}} \times \frac{\text{Girls held hands with}}{\text{Girls asked out} > 1 \text{ time}} \times \frac{\text{Girls kissed}}{\text{Girls held hands with}} \times \frac{\text{Girls proposed to}}{\text{Girls kissed}} \times \frac{\text{Girls accepted}}{\text{Girls proposed to}} = \text{Girls accepted}$$

The Profit Equation

"Doesn't it seem a little funny," Samantha says as she finishes writing the equation, "that we're writing an equation like this?"

"Yeah, I guess so," I say, trying to hide my smile. "Coach says it works for anything, so I imagine it even works for dating."

"Well," Samantha moves on, "I guess the next step is to identify the activities that will drive conversion from one piece to the next."

We talk for a few minutes about how he can get to know girls and how hard—yet necessary—it is for her brother to get up the courage to ask the girls out. Conversation then turns to how to get from one date to multiple dates.

"So what kind of a car does your brother drive?" I ask.

"What does that have to do with anything?" Samantha says with a look of puzzlement.

"Well," I begin, "don't you think he is more likely to get from the first date to multiple dates if the girls he asks out think he has some money."

"I guess it depends on the type of girl he's trying to attract," Samantha says. "But for me, it wouldn't do anything. I don't know, but it might even be a turnoff."

"Really?" I'm confused. "How so?"

"I think I want someone who isn't just out to impress me with things. I want someone who cares about me and is interested in me."

Great, I think. *Obviously, my ideas of what it takes to move from going on one date to going on multiple dates are flawed.* So, I wonder how someone shows he cares and is interested? That sounds way too complicated for me.

"So how does somebody go about showing that?" I ask.

"Oh, I don't think it's really that hard." Samantha smiles. "It's probably in the little things as much as anything. Whether a guy is wrapped up in himself or wants to talk about me and what I'm interested in. If he gets the door for me when we go places. If he gets to know my family. I haven't thought about it too much, but I don't think a guy has to have a nice car to get the girls."

That's a relief, I think to myself. Driving the El Camino, I haven't exactly seen myself as a babe magnet. I'm surprised to hear Samantha's opinion on what activities drive conversion. Compared to my view of the necessary activities, they are completely different.

"So," I say. "I'm a little embarrassed to admit this, but I totally thought the type of car a guy drives would be an important factor in helping him convert a first date into a second date. Really, what girl would want to been seen in an old El Camino like mine?"

Samantha thinks about it for a minute. "So what other types of activities do you think are important to get from a first date to a second?"

"Well," I say. "I thought a girl would be impressed if I took her to a nice place for dinner. I guess all of the ideas I had somehow related to impressing her and showing her that I had money that I would spend on her."

"Interesting," Samantha says. "So here we are with two very different ideas of what activities drive this step in the conversion process. Which one do you think is right?"

"I have no idea," I admit. "What do you think?"

"Well, suppose you are a big Raiders fan in a Broncos town, and you work at a sports store." Samantha gives me a wink. "Suppose every time someone comes into your store looking for a gift for a friend, you show them the Raiders merchandise, because that is what you would pick. How successful do you think you would be at converting people into buyers?"

"Aside from the Raiders fans, probably not too successful," I say sadly.

"Why not?" Samantha asks rhetorically. "Because you assume that the things that would convert you are the same things that would convert them. In order for the activities we choose to be successful, they have to be the activities that are converting from the convertee's point of view."

"So, how do we figure out what the convertees—as you called them—are thinking?"

"It's probably not much harder than asking them, in most cases at least. In your sports store, I'm sure you ask customers what team they like or what they are looking for, even if you would like them to buy something Raiders."

"And what about dating?" I ask. I'd like to know, or I'm doomed for sure.

"I think exactly the same way." Samantha smiles. "Say we had a date. You could ask me what kinds of things I like to do. Maybe I hate sports, but you think a night at a baseball game would be awesome. If you never ask but just take me to a game, I might come away never wanting to go out with you again. On the other hand, if you ask and find out that I love to Rollerblade, we could do that, and I'd not only have a good time, but I'd be excited to know that you cared enough to ask."

"So," I say, "say we did have a date. What kind of things do you like to do?"

We both laugh, and she tells me a few things she likes to do. Then we continue to talk through the rest of the activities for our dating equation. As we go on, I can see how critical it is to see the conversion process from the convertee's point of view.

I can't help but think that this has deeper application for our store as well. Samantha mentioned the obvious example—me offering Raiders gear to a Broncos fan—but I'm sure there are other subtle things that come into play as well. What if I were working with a Raiders fan and I was trying to sell him a jersey when what he really wants is a hat? The finding out process is critical.

The more I think about it, the more I realize that it probably differs by customer as well. Each customer has a unique activity that will convert him. The goal then must be to try to understand on a customer-by-customer basis what activities will convert that individual customer into a buyer. The more often I can understand an individual customer's needs, the more successful I will be.

Michael D. Batt

CHAPTER 22

I wake up early Wednesday and hurry to school for early morning basketball practice. Wally spends the first half of practice talking through the handful of plays that he would like us to work on before our game on Friday. He says he spent several hours after practice last night watching game film from our last game against Skyline; he talks us through why he picked the plays he did and how he thinks they will help us win our game on Friday.

We spend the rest of practice working on setting screens and shooting off of screens. He talks to us about the value of good hard screens in the different plays that we run. Wally says that if we let a man through our screens, the play goes downhill in a hurry.

It's a great practice, and I feel the hope of victory starting to grow among the guys.

The rest of the day seems to fly by. I don't see Samantha until algebra, where we only talk for a few minutes. Before we head to our next class, I tell Samantha that I've changed our plans for Saturday night. Instead of a movie, I think we'll go miniature golfing and then go skip rocks on the pond—both things that Samantha said she enjoyed doing.

Between basketball and this dating thing, I can really see the value of focusing on the end goal and then consistently pursuing the activities that will get you there. I think back to the quote in English class last week.

> Keep your mind on the great and splendid thing you would like to do; and then, as the days go gliding by, you will find

The Profit Equation

yourself unconsciously seizing the opportunities that are required for the fulfillment of your desire ... Picture in your mind the able, earnest, useful person you desire to be, and the thought that you hold is hourly transforming you into that particular individual you so admire.[3]

As we've put our equations in place, we are more than "unconsciously seizing the opportunities." We have clear pictures in our minds of the things we want to accomplish, and then we systematically identify the things that will help us accomplish our goals.

Finally, it's time to go to work. I hustle from practice to my car and then on to work. It seems like an eternity since I worked, even though it was only two nights ago. So much has happened, and I've learned a lot about this equation thing. I hope Jimmy is happy with the results.

As I roll into the parking lot at the mall, a car pulls out right next to my entrance, and I get a great spot. My luck must be changing.

The store is busy for a Wednesday night, and I throw on a jersey and get to work, without a chance to talk to Jimmy. I hope things will slow down a little before the night is over so we can walk through the process.

My mind races as I help customers. It definitely makes work more interesting as I play the game, trying to convert shoppers into buyers and then convert their orders into larger, more profitable orders. As I work with customers, I find that I am more successful at converting certain customers than I am others. After several customers, I start to see the pattern. I am naturally more successful at converting customers who are like me. They either like the teams that I like or they have similar personalities. I watch Larry, who is also working tonight and notice that the customers he is able to convert are similar to him.

---

[3] Elbert Hubbard, *Little Journeys to the Homes of the Great, Volume 5* (Project Gutenberg eBook, 2004), 131.

Michael D. Batt

How interesting. I wonder what would happen if instead of trying to work hard to improve our individual stats, we started to work together. When a Bronco fan comes into the store, I could hand him off to Larry. Likewise, when a Raiders fan comes in, I might be more suited to help him. If we can put our personal stats on the sideline and start playing as a team, we will probably be much more successful at converting more customers.

Obviously, there will be fans of teams that none of the store associates follow who will come into the store. So how do we handle those customers? I start thinking about why I am successful with Raiders fans. I know the names of the players on the team. I know their records. I know who they play next.

I bet if I were to spend some time really paying attention to some other teams and finding out more about them, I would be more successful in selling to more people. I make a mental note that learning about other teams will be an activity that I can perform that will help me convert more people.

I spend the next half hour trying it out. Each time a customer comes into the store, I pretend to be a fan of their team. I ask a lot of questions, trying to sound intelligent without giving away the fact that I don't know much. I'm surprised to see people open up and talk about last week's game, their favorite players, why they love or hate the coach, and ultimately end up buying something.

Now that I'm on the hunt, I'm sure there are other little things that we could do to make this more of a science. I notice, for example, that in many instances we've put merchandise together by style or type—the T-shirts are with the T-shirts, the hats are with the hats. When a Chargers fan comes in, I spend half my time running around looking for what we have available in that team, only to find the item they probably would have bought long after they've left the store. What if we were to merchandise the store based on team as much as possible to make the conversion process more streamlined?

The rest of the night we stay pretty busy with the customers in the store. By the time the night is over, I've smoked Larry and

The Profit Equation

Jimmy in sales. Jimmy is anxious to figure out how I did it. He asks Larry to count the tills while we go into the backroom to talk.

Before we start, Jimmy informs me that the DM called today and is planning on spending the day with us on Saturday to see what kind of progress we've made. I explain that I think I have just the answer we need. With that, I erase the beloved stat board, and we get down to work.

"Jimmy," I begin, "remember on Monday when we were working? A man came into the store who had recently been converted to a church. You told me that some of the stores in the mall, from time to time, measure conversion rate?"

"Yeah, I remember," Jimmy says. "If I remember right, that's when you took off and said you had the answer but needed some time to think about it."

"That's right." I smile.

"So, tell me what you've learned,." Jimmy urges impatiently. "With the DM coming on Saturday, we need to put up a couple of big days if we really want him to pay attention."

I spend the next several minutes walking through the process of building *The Profit Equation* with Jimmy. I write it all out the way I did yesterday.

$$\text{Customers} \times \frac{\text{Transactions}}{\text{Customers}} \times \frac{\text{Items}}{\text{Transactions}} \times \frac{\text{Sales}}{\text{Items}} \times \frac{(\text{Sales} - \text{Costs})}{\text{Sales}} = \text{Profit}$$

"So, what does this equation have to do with making our store click?" Jimmy asks. "We measure some of these things already."

"That's true; we do," I say. "The difference is that now we are going to have all of the pieces of the puzzle, whereas before, we were trying to make it happen with only a few pieces. We also have a better understanding of how all of the pieces go together to make the whole. Now we don't measure *Items per Transaction* just to measure *Items per Transaction*. We measure *Items per Transaction* in order to explain one piece of our total *Profit Equation*."

"I buy that, but how will that make us do things any differently than we do now?"

"Well, building the equation is only the first part of the process. Let's talk for a minute about conversion."

"You mean how many people we can get to buy?" Jimmy asks.

"That's part of it. That's what got me thinking in the first place. In order to get to *Profit*, we have to do some conversions," I explain. "The first conversion is the one you mentioned—changing customers into buyers. Once we do that, we then have to convert those transactions into more profitable transactions. We do that by adding items and by adding more expensive items."

"Okay, so maybe I'm dumb, but I'm not following where you're going with this. What is so different about this than what we are currently doing, trying to sell more items and more expensive items?"

"Well," I think about how to explain it, "it's really not that different. The key is that our ultimate goal is to drive *Profit*—not *Items per Transaction* or *Average Sale*. When we focus on the individual stats, we lose sight of the real end goal. Potentially we start playing games that will boost the individual stats but may actually be harmful to the end result."

I walk Jimmy through the example of the jewelry store and the inexpensive high volume store that are across the hall from each other in a mall. We talk about how the two different stores use the same equation but different pieces of the equation to drive their profitability. I explain that if either store loses sight of their ultimate goal and strategy and starts to focus on an individual stat, that store may end up gaining local optimization for that one stat at the sacrifice of profitability.

"I think I'm starting to understand." Jimmy nods as I finish my example. "So my question then is how do we decide which strategy we should pursue and how do we make these conversions happen consistently?"

"Great questions." I grin. "That leads us to the next step of the process. As for which strategy to pursue, it's partially a function of the industry, I think. There's probably no single answer. Just thinking out loud, I'd guess that the important thing is to pick a strategy and then stick with it. As for how to make the conversions happen consistently, we have to identify what activities will convert the customers from one stage to the next. I'll show you what I mean."

I go to the board and write "Activities" under each of the multiplication symbols. I list a few activities and then ask Jimmy what he thinks. He comes up with some more ideas. I explain to him the lesson I learned with Samantha about trying to impress her with the things that would impress me. I also share the secret of my success tonight—trying to put myself in the customers' shoes and convert them through the things that motivate them.

We talk through the inventory selection, the arrangement of the merchandise in the store, our sales staff—even down to the cleaning schedule and how a clean store might help convert more people. It seems like the list could keep going forever.

When it seems like we have a pretty good list, Jimmy asks which activities we should focus on first. As I noticed before with the basketball equation, it becomes apparent that there are certain activities that show up under multiple conversion points. Better inventory selection is one. A more attentive sales staff is another.

Jimmy starts to give me reasons why we can't increase our inventory levels to carry more inventory—we have to sell through our inventory a certain number of times each year; we can't fit any more in the store; we have minimums that we have to purchase on certain items. As he goes on about the various constraints, it reminds me that we haven't listed the boundaries yet.

I stop him and explain the boundaries list. It seems like there are plenty. Jimmy lists all of the excuses he has received when he's asked for different things at different times. Some of them are legitimate; others I think could be questioned.

We list as many of the boundaries as we can think of. Then we go through the list and circle the ones that seem to be hindering us from completing conversions at one step of the process or another. We start to brainstorm ways that we might be able to tear down those hurdles.

Once we get going, Jimmy really buys into the idea. He likes the idea that we can tie a lot of the activities that we already do—even some of the unpleasant ones like cleaning the store—into converting activities. Just like with my basketball team, it seems to give the activities an additional sense of purpose. If we can explain how a clean store will help us sell more merchandise, he hopes it will cut down on some of the griping as well as motivate the guys to be a little more thorough in their jobs.

As we continue to talk through the process, Jimmy asks, "So one last question. What should we measure going forward? I'm sold on the equation and the value of looking at all of the pieces. I'm concerned that we start to measure too many things."

"That was one of my concerns as well: that we'd get too focused on the pieces or the activities again. I think to really make this work, you have to reward on what you actually want—in this case, profits. If you measure and reward on the pieces, you will ultimately get the pieces. No question. You may or may not get the whole, though."

"So what about the pieces?" Jimmy asks. "Do we not measure them at all?"

"Oh, I definitely think we measure them. Instead of being the end though, they now become a means to the end. We have to use the pieces to help us get to the whole. The individual measurements serve more like tools, helping us figure out how to accomplish the overall result. In the end, we measure and reward on store profitability, because that is what we want."

"Okay, one more question. If we are focused now on this overall store goal, how do we make sure we don't have slackers who are riding on the coattails of others?" Jimmy asks.

"I imagine it will be easier than you think," I assure him. "Just think if you were hired with a group of guys to complete a large construction project. If you were told that you would be rewarded as a group when the job was done—but only if it were

The Profit Equation

done by a certain time—what would happen if certain members of the team weren't pulling their weight?"

"I'd be all over them," Jimmy says. "If their effort directly impacts my payout, I'd make sure everyone was busting it."

"And if they didn't?"

"I'd want them off of the crew."

"So," I go on, "what you're saying is that the leader wouldn't have to do much supervising at all?"

"Yeah, I guess not. The team would probably unite and supervise themselves, encouraging each other and weeding out the slackers."

"Exactly. Managers don't think that us lowly part-timers care at all about the big picture, and they think that we definitely won't be motivated by it. In actuality, I'd love to feel like the team depended on me to make it happen, especially if I was getting rewarded for it."

"Well," Jimmy says, smiling, "That sure sounds like it would make my job a lot easier. I spend half my time trying to get some of the guys motivated. I'm willing to give it a try."

"Great. So when can we start?"

"How about right now? Let's go see if Larry is finished and is willing to be our guinea pig."

We stand up, and I take off my jersey and hang it in the backroom. As we walk out into the store, Jimmy remembers one more question.

"So what about inventory levels and inventory shrink? Those are two things the merchandise purchasers are always monitoring. How do they fit into the equation?"

"Well, for starters, they are both costs that would impact our overall profitability. Inventory has a cost to carry it. Inventory shrink is also definitely a cost—the more you lose, the more you have to replace. Beyond that, they may also be included on our list of boundaries."

"Oh yeah?" Jimmy sounds surprised. "How so?"

"Well, say we have all of the cash we need, so purchasing the inventory isn't an issue. We may determine, however, that having too much inventory on hand is a risk that we need to monitor. We may decide that, if we have over a certain amount of inventory on hand, we are exposed to a greater risk if styles change or if, in our case, a player gets traded. So we may decide that $150,000 in inventory is the boundary for our inventory to control our risk. This would, however, have to be a boundary that we watch closely. If we decide that we can increase our sales significantly by crossing that boundary, we may want to change it. Ultimately, we have to maximize our profit while mitigating our risk where possible."

"Okay." Jimmy seems satisfied for the meantime.

We make our way up to the counter, where Larry is just finishing up. We talk through the process with Larry, and he agrees to give it a try, especially when we tell him that he won't have to help as many Raiders fans anymore.

He's a little concerned that he might not get the recognition he has received before for his great stats, but he admits that the model makes sense and will probably increase our store sales.

As we lock up the store, Jimmy is excited to see what will happen.

"It's been a bit of a drag coming to work the last few weeks, knowing that my job is on the line. I'm excited to see if we can make this work."

"I'm sure it will," I assure him. "After all, Coach H. is the mastermind behind this process, and if he can win state in baseball with the team he did, we can do anything."

Jimmy slaps me on the back and smiles as we walk out to the parking lot together. "I sure hope so, Davis. I sure hope so."

Chapter 23

The next few days go by in a blur. We bust our tails in basketball practice, doing our best to master the activities that will help us maximize our possessions and then convert our possessions into the most total points.

By the time Friday rolls around, we are firing on all pistons. For the most part, the guys are focused on the good of the whole and are resolved not to worry about their individual stats or points. Of course, old habits die hard, and now and again, we have to reign somebody in when he starts hogging the ball.

We suit up before the game, and Wally walks us through the game plan one more time. Read the defense, run our plays, and play tough defense. We have to stop them from maximizing their equation while we do our best to run our conversion from one piece to the next.

When we take the court, we're a completely different team than the team we put on the floor two weeks ago. We are ready to work as a team and see if we can make it happen. Skyline comes out early, and instead of the man-to-man defense we were expecting, they throw a zone defense at us. Luckily, Wally had talked us through this before the game. In the past, we would have pushed ahead and tried to run a few plays that we were only mediocre at executing. After a few trips up and down the court, we would give up, because they weren't working and start playing like kids on the playground—every man for himself.

This time it's different. Every possession matters. We focus on having every possession result in a shot as opposed to a turnover. We work on executing our plays and setting good screens to turn every shot we take into a shot we make. As we read their defense, we focus on making more three-pointers to increase the overall value of the shots we are making.

At one point in the game, we realize that we have a mismatch down under. Our strong forward Jeff is matched up with a smaller guy who is a few inches shorter than he is. While Jeff is a good shot, he really hasn't scored much during the games we've played, mostly because Slim and I are better all-around shooters, so we usually take the majority of the shots. With our new mindset though, we are all about conversion. We start feeding the ball inside to Jeff and he makes four or five buckets in a row.

Skyline starts to scramble and switches up their defense to man-to-man and takes one of their better defenders off of Slim to guard Jeff. We read the move—just like I'd read a customer in the store—and switch up our plays to feed Slim. Instead of forcing something that only works some of the time, we focus on driving our conversions toward the goal of maximizing our total points—in any way that we can.

When the final buzzer sounds, we've trounced them. It's a complete turnaround from the beating we received at their hands only a few weeks ago. With the victory, we now have a slot in the district tournament. We'll run up against some tough teams—including Skyline again—but I'm sure things will work out if we can focus on making our equation work.

After I get cleaned up, I make my way out of the locker room and am surprised to see Samantha waiting for me.

"Great game, Andy!" Samantha smiles and waves.

"Thanks," I say, smiling back. "I didn't play that well, but we pulled off a win."

"Are you kidding?" Samantha grins, "You were great! You kept the team focused on driving your equation. It was cool to watch it unfold from the stands. They never knew what hit them. They'd probably laugh if somebody told them they were beat by a little algebra in action."

The Profit Equation

"I guess you're right. Everybody really caught the vision and stayed focused on reaching our end goal."

As we talk, the guys start to file out of the locker room.

"Great game, Davis," Slim hollers as he comes through the doors. "All the way to state, baby!"

"Easy, Slim," I say. "Remember, one piece at time."

"Sure, Davis." Slim slaps me on the back. "Whatever you say, math man."

I grin and slap him back as the guys head out to the parking lot. Wally promised to take us to dinner, so everyone's headed over to Molly's.

"Well, I better get going, Samantha. We're meeting for dinner with the team, and then I need to get ready for a big day at work tomorrow," I tell her. "The DM's coming to see how we're doing. Jimmy called last night and said they've put up some pretty solid sales numbers the last couple of days. He's called the DM and prepped him that we have something to show him. I hope it all goes well—for Jimmy's sake."

"I'm sure it will," Samantha reassures me. "After all, you are the math man."

We both laugh.

"Are we still on for tomorrow night?" I ask as we walk out to the parking lot together.

"You bet." Samantha smiles. "I can't wait."

I open her door and help her into her car. Once I'm back in my car, I turn on the radio to listen to the post-game commentary. The announcers can't say enough about the unbelievable change that came over us tonight compared to our performance during the last match up with Skyline. They'd never believe it was algebra that made the difference.

The guys are pretty excited when I finally show up at Molly's. We talk through the game as we gorge ourselves on pizza. After the celebration, Wally walks us through the final stats of the game. We had more possessions than we usually have and didn't have any one player who scored more than twelve points. It was an all-around balanced attack—and it worked!

Chapter 24

As Jimmy and I work on straightening a few things up the next day at work, we talk through the equation. Jimmy has clearly spent some time thinking it over since we talked on Wednesday, and he has really bought into it.

He even went out Thursday morning, bought a customer counter, and installed it at the entrance of our store. Each hour, he checks it to see how many customers have come into the store. He calculates the *Conversion Rate*, the *Items per Transaction*, the *Average Price of Items Sold*, and the *Margin* on each sale. He's decided that, for the purpose of the daily calculations, that is as far as he will go—just measuring the contribution margin, or profit before the expenses like rent and labor, that the store is making. At the end of each month, he will take the rest of the expenses and see what our overall profit is.

Jimmy took down the stat board in the back and has replaced it with a blown-up version of our equation. He admits that it's a little risky abandoning the stat board when the DM is coming today, but he feels pretty confident that he can win him over. In the backroom of the store, he has an overall profit goal for the month as well as a margin goal for the month. He's broken down the goal on a daily basis so we know what we need to do each day.

He met with the rest of the staff on Thursday night and walked them through the process. He assures me that everyone is willing to give it a try. Based on the sales for the last two days, it appears to be working. They were the biggest Thursday and Friday we've had in several months.

When the DM finally arrives, he comes in, and after a little casual conversation, he jumps on the computer and starts looking back through the past few days of stats.

"Jimmy," he begins, "I thought I told you to increase your stats—not drive them into the ground. From what I see here, your *Average Sale* for the last few days has bottomed out, not to mention your *IPT* stinks. What's going on?"

It's now or never, I think. I hope Jimmy doesn't blow it.

"Check out our sales the last few days," Jimmy says, "We put up a couple of the best days we've had in months."

"Yeah, but think how much better they would have been if you would have had at least company average stats."

"What if I were to tell you that I think the stats we measure—*Average Sale* and *IPT*—are only parts of the equation to making our store tick? Would you believe me that part of the magic of making our overall sales increase the last two days was by intentionally lowering our *Average Sale* and *IPT*?"

"No," the DM says, "I don't think I would believe you."

"Will you at least give me a chance to explain, if for no other reason than for the fact that we smoked all of the other stores in the company for the last two days and I think we have the key to make it work across the board?"

The DM is skeptical, but he agrees to hear Jimmy out. Jimmy leads him into the backroom and seems to be there for an eternity as Larry and I hold down the floor. We work our magic on the customers as they come through the door. Larry handles the ladies and the Broncos fans—those seem to be his specialty—while I focus on the Raiders fans and the guys. Every once in a while, he comes across a customer who just doesn't seem to jive with his style. Where he would have pushed ahead with the sale before, he tries to hand them off to me to see if I'll have any better luck.

Overall, our new sales technique is working better. We do our best to help every customer, even if it only results in a $5 keychain sale. Now that we have expanded our efforts beyond a few isolated metrics and are focused on the whole, things really seem to click. Larry cringes occasionally when a small sale comes through, and he watches his personal stats sink, but overall, he's hanging tight with me in sales, something he surely didn't do last Saturday.

Finally Jimmy and the DM emerge from the backroom. Jimmy leads him to the front of the store and shows him the customer counter and then shows him the sheet at the counter where he has been tracking our stats.

"So what you're saying, Jimmy, is that, in order to maximize the company profits, we have to move away from this local optimization that is caused by focusing on individual stats and really focus on the whole equation and the activities that make it move?"

"That's right," Jimmy says, beaming. I can tell that the conversation ended pretty well, even though the morning started a little rough.

"It makes sense," the DM says as he leans against the counter and studies the sheet Jimmy has made to track the stats.

"So what do you guys think?" The DM asks as he turns his attention to Larry and me.

"As long as I can avoid talking to Raiders fans," Larry answers first, "I'm all about it."

"What do you mean?"

"Well," Larry says, smiling, "Davis here loves the Raiders, so I let him work his magic on them. I focus my efforts on the Broncos fans and the ladies."

"Like I was explaining in the backroom," Jimmy says, "as we focus on maximizing overall profits, one of the activities that we identified as being key in driving the conversions from *Customers* to *Profit*, is trying to match customers with employees who are most suited to meet their needs. Davis is a huge Raiders fan, so we try to funnel Raiders fans his way. Larry works on the Broncos fans. At the same time, we are making a committed effort to expand our knowledge and understanding about all of the different teams, so eventually we will all be able to help any customer effectively. I imagine there will still be certain customers who mesh with one

The Profit Equation

employee better than another. We've only been doing this for a few days, so we'll have to adjust as we go."

The DM continues to study the sheet without saying much. I honestly don't know how someone can't buy into the process if he really gets it.

"So, I'd like to see this in action today. Tell me what I ought to do."

Jimmy is beaming from ear to ear as he finds out which teams the DM likes. We then talk through the project we want to work on today as we have time—remerchandising the store to cluster like teams together as much as possible. We hope this will increase our likelihood of converting a customer when she sees our whole selection of merchandise for her team in one place.

We get to work and, by one thirty, have hit our profit goal for the day. The DM is clearly impressed. During a midafternoon lull, we start talking.

"We need a better selection on some of the teams if we are really going to turn more shoppers into buyers," the DM admits.

"No kidding," I agree quickly. "We've been trying to tell people that for months. Jimmy says the problem is we have a limit on the amount of inventory we can carry in the stores."

"Yeah, that's an ongoing concern for the buyers, who really focus on turning over their inventory so many times a year. My question is 'Why do we have six medium Broncos sweatshirts?' We can't sell that many over the course of a month."

I remind him that that is the minimum order quantity, and given the fact that we drop ship all of our merchandise, we have to get that many at a time if we want to carry the style at all.

"There have to be ways to work around that," the DM says. "I'll have to go back to the home office and see what we can work out. If we could take those dollars and spend them on a broader selection, it would probably increase our conversion rate—not to mention our *Average Sale* and *IPT*, since people would have more selection to choose from. Let's see what I can do."

I guess that's another good example of breaking down boundaries. It's not that the boundary isn't valid, but it's the way we are playing within the boundary that is giving us problems. I'm excited to see what can happen if we can really get the DM and the home office on board.

After we work for a while longer, the DM speaks up again.

"Davis, I hear that you're the mastermind behind this new *Profit Equation* thing. I really think you have something here. As I try to run this up the flagpole at corporate, I'd love to have you help out if I get stuck with something I'm not sure how to explain. Is that something you'd be willing to do?"

"Sure," I say. What else can I say? "I don't know that I have all of the answers, but I think we can figure them out."

"Sounds good. Based on what I've seen in just these few hours, I think our VP of operations would love to get in on this deal. It has huge potential."

We continue to work through the afternoon, and when I leave at six so I can clean up for my date tonight, we are 215 percent over our goal for the day. Jimmy is pumped, and the DM is pretty pleased with the way things went today.

"Thanks for everything," Jimmy says as I head out the door.

"No problem," I say. "I'm excited to see what we can do, not to mention I'm glad I still have a job."

I hurry out to the parking lot and rush home. I clean up, and by six forty-five, I'm pulling up to Samantha's house. After all the time I've spent with her, you wouldn't think I'd be nervous, but something about a first date gives me the jitters.

I'm still a little self-conscious about my old beater car, but Samantha said she doesn't care, so I'll have to take her word for it. I walk to the door and ring the doorbell. Mr. Wilmington answers the door, shows me into the living room, and offers me a seat.

"Samantha will be down in a minute or two." Mr. Wilmington says as he sits down in the easy chair across from me. "Congratulations on your big win last night. Samantha said you guys played great."

"It was a fun game. Things finally are coming together for us." I'm never exactly sure how to graciously accept compliments.

"Well, I hope you guys can continue to win. I'd love to see you make it to the state tournament. It's been a while since our team has made it that far."

"That's what we're shooting for," I say. "I think, if we can keep it going, we've got a pretty good chance of going quite a ways."

"Old Wally sure deserves it. He's put his heart into that team for a lot of years. I'd love to see him come away with at least one championship."

"He's a good coach. We'll see what we can do."

At that, Samantha comes down the stairs. Mr. Wilmington and I stand up as she comes into the living room. She looks great—as always. She also seems genuinely happy to see me, which helps alleviate some of my anxiety about our date.

"Ready to go, Andy?" Samantha asks.

"You bet."

Mr. Wilmington opens the front door for us and stands in the doorway as we walk down the path to my car.

"You two have fun and don't stay out too late," he calls after us. He watches as I open Samantha's door for her and help her in and then go around to my side of the car. Nothing like having your date's father watching to turn up the pressure.

We head to the miniature golf course across town, and for the first time we talk about something besides algebra and equations as we drive. It's great.

Samantha really takes it to me at miniature golf and beats me soundly. No wonder she likes it—she's a pro. We laugh and joke as we play and have a lot of fun. This is definitely better than going to the movies.

I'm not exactly sure what she'd like to eat, but after worrying about it while we play golf, I decide that the best way to find out would be to ask—a lesson learned from Samantha. We decide to grab some food at a fast-food place and then head over to the park to eat. We walk around for a few minutes, looking for a good picnic table. We pick one near the pond so we can watch the ducks. We eat and talk about all that has happened in the last few weeks. It's been quite a ride.

For the most part, we are well on our way to conquering problems that seemed unconquerable a few weeks ago. I never could have believed that I'd ever enjoy math—let alone actually use it to solve my problems.

When we finish eating, we skip rocks on the pond. It's a perfect first date! We sit and talk as the sun sets.

As we drive home, I debate whether or not I should ask Samantha to go out again next week. I think she had a good time, but I'm not positive. Now that we've figured the whole equation thing out, maybe she won't want to hang out anymore. I guess this is where the discipline is necessary to carry through on the activities that will convert from one piece of the equation to the next.

"Samantha," I start, when there's a pause in the conversation. "I was wondering—if you don't already have other plans—if you'd like to go out again next week. We could go bowling or take four-wheelers out to the sand dunes or something."

"I'd love to, Andy," Samantha says.

We smile at each other, realizing without saying anything that we've just made the conversion to the next step in our process. If she realizes that we're now working on this equation and still said yes, she must really be okay with the idea.

Chapter 25

Monday morning, I show up at school a little early in the hope of catching Coach H. before class starts. I want to report on the success I've had and find out what else I need to do.

When I pull in, I see Coach's mustang in its regular spot. I hurry into the school and down the hall to his classroom.

Coach is sitting at his desk, working on something.

"Coach," I interrupt him. "Mind if I come in?"

"Not at all, Davis." Coach puts away what he's working on and stands up as I walk in. "Great game on Friday, Davis." He grins. "It looks like it's working. Do you think you can keep it rolling?"

"As long as we stick to the equation, I think we can do it, Coach." I don't think I've sounded that confident in a long time about our basketball team—or probably about anything for that matter. I've really changed my perspective on a lot of things in the past few weeks.

"So how's everything else going?" Coach asks.

"Better than you'd believe, Coach," I say. "Who would have thought that just a week or two ago we were having this same conversation and I felt like everything was in shambles? Now I feel like I have some direction and some tools to really handle my problems."

"See, what did I tell you?" Coach beams; I realize that's exactly what he said could happen. "Algebra really is the tool to restore the broken parts."

I fill Coach in about work and about my day on Saturday with the DM. Then he asks about Samantha. I give him the update on the latest progress on our equation.

"So what's next, Coach?" I ask. "Where do I go from here?"

"You know what you need to know, Davis. From here on out, it's just a matter of refining your equations so they're complex enough to explain the different pieces of your puzzle but simple enough to really drive the behavior that will get you to your final result. I think you'll find, too, that several of the activities that you've identified will need to be tweaked and adjusted until you really fine-tune the process of driving conversion toward your final goal.

"With time, some of the activities may change a little, but you'll be surprised how resilient your equations will be. No more changing metrics every quarter in search of the answer that will solve your problems. If you get the equation right, it can serve as an anchor for you to make sure you really stay focused on the things that matter—no matter what your problem may be."

"So that's it, huh?" I ask. "Now that we've been through the process, it almost seems too simple to be true. Identify the goal, figure out the pieces, and put the puzzle together. Then identify the activities that drive the equation, set the boundaries you have to work within, and go to work. I wonder why I never figured this out on my own."

"You did, Davis." Coach smiles. "I gave you a few tips along the way, but you really did figure it out on your own."

"Well, we couldn't have figured it out without you. Thanks for your help, Coach."

"No problem, Davis," Coach says. "That's the fun part of being a teacher—when your students really get it and then find a use for the things you're trying to teach them."

"So, Coach," I say. I just remembered something. "When we first talked a few weeks ago, you said you'd tell me sometime how you ended up being so good at math. How 'bout it? How did a college baseball player end up in a high school algebra classroom?"

The Profit Equation

"You probably won't believe it, but remember when I told you that, at one point, I was exactly in your shoes? I was playing baseball in college. Third baseman. I had every intention in the world of playing major league baseball someday. I wanted to graduate from college first though and had to take Algebra 101 as a required class.

"I was working at the mall in my little college town trying to fill in the gap where my partial-ride baseball scholarship fell short. I had a crush on this girl but didn't have the guts to ask her out."

Coach leans back in his chair and smiles as he thinks back to the good old days.

"Besides having a few scouts looking at me, things were on pretty shaky ground. I wasn't sure I could pass algebra, which I had to do to stay eligible. I had a boss who was a jerk and was always riding me to get my stats up.

"One day in algebra, my teacher had a little heart-to-heart with the class. He told us about the power of algebra … really a lot of the same stuff that I've been telling you. Over the course of a couple of weeks, he walked us through the process that you've just learned.

"Something clicked for me. It all made sense, and I saw the beauty of it. I was still determined to play major league baseball, but I could see the power of focusing on a goal and then mapping out a way to get there.

"I started making equations for everything. My job improved, I passed algebra, and I ended up marrying that girl I had a crush on.

"When I tore my rotator cuff, the doctors said I had to lay off baseball—and that I'd never make it in the pros. It took me a while to pick myself up from that blow, but when I did, I started thinking about what I could do with my life. All I ever wanted to do was play baseball.

"With a little urging from my college algebra teacher, I finally decided to teach algebra. He told me that there are only a handful of people who get the power of algebra and then make it work in their lives. He said he saw it in me and said I could do a world of good by passing the power on to others, like you and Samantha.

"So, here I am. A high school algebra teacher and baseball coach."

"So what you're saying," I say, "is that you knew the answers to my questions all along? You'd already built these equations, and you made me build 'em again."

"Sure." Coach leans forward. "It wouldn't have meant nearly as much to you if you hadn't figured it out on your own."

He's probably right, but I still think I could have appreciated it if he would have just told me the answers.

I stand up and head for the door.

"Thanks for all the help, Coach. I'm sure I still have a lot to learn, so I'll probably be back. I almost wish I had a few more problems so I could practice a little more."

"Don't worry. They'll come fast enough," Coach assures me.

As I reach the door, Coach calls from his desk, "So Davis, have you ever thought about being an algebra teacher? There's only a handful of people who really get the power of algebra. I think you've got it. You can do a lot of good by passing it on to others."

I smile and tell him I'll think about it. A few weeks ago, I would have laughed out loud, but now I don't know. Maybe it would be something I could enjoy.

About the Author

Michael Batt lives and works in Idaho Falls, Idaho. He graduated with a bachelor's degree from Brigham Young University's accounting program and an MBA from the University of Utah. He worked for many years with the National Basketball Association's Utah Jazz in their retail division in roles including controller, e-commerce manager, vice president and general manager.

Subsequently, Michael has worked as a sr. financial analyst and the marketing services manager for the direct-to-consumer marketing company, Melaleuca, and as the chief operating officer and then general manager of Riverbend Holdings—a company that has operations including ranching, real estate investment, radio broadcasting, construction and title insurance.

His favorite past time is spending time with his wife, Anne, and their five wonderful children.